THE FLASHING STREAM

COPYRIGHT

TO
MARGARET RAWLINGS

CONTENTS

FOREWORD

FOREWORD

I HAVE been a little reluctant to attach to this play a preface that may seem to overweight it, and I hope that a few readers may be willing to regard *The Flashing Stream* as a pendant to the essay that now precedes it.

It was written during a month's holiday spent beside Llangorse Lake, in Breconshire, in the summer of 1937. I had come there with the unfinished manuscript of a novel, and had intended, during my holiday, to continue it, but I found that I had reached a period of the narrative and could not proceed without an interval in which ideas should mature and imagination be refreshed. It is a peculiarity in me—whether for good or evil, it is hard to say—that I imagine more intensely on paper than when I am idle. The written sheet is a focal point for the mind ; the pen's sound excludes all others ; together they produce that happy concentration which gives to the craft of writing and the everlasting patience implied in it an underlying " lift " and joy, so that, while a relative clause is being pared away, ideas " come of themselves ", a tangle is shaken out. The subject that engrossed me, on my novel's account, was singleness of mind. I needed a holiday task that bore upon it, and *The Flashing Stream*, which I had turned over in my thought long ago, reappeared to supply my need. No one who has not spent eight years of his life in composing two long narratives can know what delight there is in attacking a play which will yield a rough draft in four weeks.

The Flashing Stream was written fast because stage-dialogue ought to be written fast, but has since been elaborately revised. Its subject is singleness of mind and an aspect of love. I am aware that it reflects only a part of its dual subject ; but it is true by my own standards of truth ; it throws out no sops ; its background of naval officers doing their work is one that interests me and of which I have had personal experience. A play is useless that does not reach its audience, and the audience of what is called a " west-end " theatre is not the easiest before which to express, in the naturalistic convention, the idea implicit in the sixth beatitude. If the piece fails on the stage, the fault will not be in its interpreters. No beginner in the theatre, and, I think, no dramatist, has ever come nearer to obtaining the players of his choice, and certainly none has enjoyed the collaboration of an actor-manager more patient of authors or more creatively and unselfishly loyal to his material than Mr. Godfrey Tearle. If the play fails, it will fail because the audience, collectively slower in mind than the individuals who compose it, feel that its thought and passion are over-compressed. I shall not blame them. This peril attends all modern dramatists whose subject is complex or challenging, and who cannot afford time to provoke an easy laugh every six lines. It is a peril we must accept, and accept without scorn or whining or self-righteousness.

There is, nevertheless, a temptation to supplement in a preface the extreme compression of the stage. Of singleness of mind I have written in the essay that follows; of the particular aspect of love represented in Edward Ferrers and Karen Selby something may be said here. It will be observed that, though they love each other at sight, they subordinate their personal desires to the work they have in common, and do not lie together while the nature and circumstances of that work require that they devote themselves wholly to it with " impersonal passion " and singleness of mind. An American reader has objected that so much restraint is " non-adult " ; he was unable to understand why two people who desired each other did not at once satisfy their desire. In England, those who were the " moderns " of 1922 and survive to-day as the Chromium Plated school of manners, will share this American's view. For their sake it may be said that Ferrers and Karen Selby refrained for three reasons. First, she was joining Ferrers' unit as the equivalent of an officer under his command, and there are evident disadvantages in confusing a disciplinary relationship with that of lover and mistress. Second, they were about to share the lives of men not naturally, but by compulsion, celibate. Third, they knew, not as sentimentalists but as realists, that the experience of sex is not what the Chromium Platers pretended in 1922 that it was and still pretend that it is : unimportant except as an ephemeral pleasure. It may be, at any rate for a time, an enemy of singleness of mind. A great part of a man's life, particularly if he be a man of genius, depends upon a woman's appearing in his monastery. The question presents itself : does she, perhaps subconsciously, seek to destroy his work, feeling that it excludes her ? She

says she does not ; often, like Lady Helston, she believes
that she wishes to inspire his work—a belief to be taken
with a grain of salt, for, while there are many eager to
inspire, there are few who can or will by patience, abstin-
ence, self-effacement and the lifting of all demands, give
opportunity to the work inspired. It is not that chastity
itself is necessary to singleness of mind but that unchastity
implies, in most human beings, commitments that are
destructive. To men of ideas, ideas are like the young
of white mice. They appear often and without great
difficulty, but, if they are disturbed, their parents have a
tendency to eat them before they grow up. To take a
mistress is to risk disturbance, for though there are many
loving and unselfish women in the world who will submit
their interest and devote their lives to men of ideas, there
are few whose submission includes a willingness to be
sometimes forgotten. For this fact they are not to be
blamed, but it remains a fact. Women of ideas, who
have their own work to do and their own singleness of
mind to preserve, recognize, as its converse, that men,
when they are lovers, insist upon being remembered.

For these reasons Ferrers and Karen abstain. To the
materialists of 1922, they are not valid reasons, for, they
argue, commitment may be avoided by promiscuity.
In a fortress to which but two women were admitted,
Ferrers, with the worst will in the world, might have
found it hard to be promiscuous. Apart from this con-
sideration of scarcity, his reasons are endorsed by human
experience. The Chromium Platers are caught in their
own trap. They declared that the experience of sex was
unimportant because they wished promiscuously to

indulge in it. Now that by their promiscuity they have made it meaningless to themselves except as a drug, they call " non-adult ", and affect a defensive contempt for, all who have preserved what they have lost—the romanticism of their predecessors, the selective courage of men and women younger than themselves. They claim still to be modern because they have never come out of the ditch where they hoisted, nearly twenty years ago, a modernist flag ; but, in fact, they have never been in the line of development of contemporary ideas on sex. Their fathers knew better before them ; their sons know better to-day ; and there is a connexion between the sexual ethic of the past and that of the present which does not include the 1922 generation even as a link. The notion that a man and a girl who love each other are necessarily fools if they abstain from or postpone their lying together was not accepted before the war and is not accepted by the young to-day. It is accepted by no one but the Chromium Plated group, whose stale and barren influence happens to be powerful in the commercial theatre of London and New York. It is partly for this reason that *The Flashing Stream* has been written. Certainly for this reason it will be attacked.

Another question presents itself in the person of Karen Selby. She is exceptional in intellect, for she is a mathematician of the first rank, and she knows, of her own knowledge, the nature and value of the singleness of mind that Ferrers wishes to preserve. She is not, I believe, exceptional in her attitude towards love, though the truth which she admits openly is one that has not hitherto been recognized in the modern theatre. It is remarkable that the theatre should still conventionally hide it, for it is a simple and not shameful truth which has always existed and upon which the continuance of the race depends—namely, that many women (though not, perhaps, so great a proportion of women as of men) have pleasure in the experience of sex. In life this is known ; in all serious writing on sex and in all novels that pretend to honesty and truth, it is admitted ; there is probably not an intelligent woman living who would deny it ; and yet to acknowledge its truth in what is called the heroine of a play is almost revolutionary. Shaw has done invaluable service in breaking down by his ridicule many conventions with which Robertson, Pinero and Jones surrounded the women of their theatre, but the passionate aspect of love has not engaged his intellect and he has allowed to stand unchallenged the Pinerotic theory that a woman, to be entitled to our respect in the theatre, must, if she shares a man's bed, do so with a self-sacrificial reluctance. There are, in the modern theatre, innumerable instances, in farce or light comedy, of promiscuous or greedy or sexually frivolous women whose company the adult Chromium Platers are invited to enjoy ; but dramatists who hope to strike a compromise between serious portraiture and the prejudices of fashionable sentiment have for many years spent their skill in ascribing to their heroines' unchastity every cause except the natural one. Their heroines—and even their villainesses— have yielded, when they have yielded at all, for reasons so far removed from their own desires that one might be led to believe, if there were no other than theatrical evidence, that women were all natural celibates. They consented for the sake of a title, or for money, or because a wicked man had possession of an incriminating document, or to save their uncle from a Chinese torturer, or —*consule Barrie*—because they felt maternal towards the young man who proposed to them. Sometimes, indeed, heroines were rash enough to marry because they were " in love ", but the phrase was used with no more implication of desire than is to be heard in the word " check " when spoken over a chess-board ; it was a recognized means of threatening one's opponent and of bringing the game to a conclusion. The heroine left her mamma's house without a stain on her niceness. If she reappeared in the next act with a baby, one assumed, for lack of evidence to the contrary, that she had " given herself ", and her husband was expected to act upon this theory, treating her as though he had committed a crime that it was his duty to expiate. Meanwhile, the bystanders, by their reticences, put as much blame as possible on the stork. The one thing certain in the theatre was that no romantic heroine who confessed to Juliet's warmth of feeling could hope to retain the sympathy of her audience. This convention persists, and Karen Selby challenges it. The play may well disappoint the box-office for that reason.

By some Karen will be treated with suspicion, because, though she loves Ferrers, she swerves towards Brissing at a moment when she doubts Ferrers' love for her. By strict theatrical convention, a heroine, once " in love ", is supposed to become unaware that men are men and to be chaste without effort. In life this is not so. A woman is vitalized and made more than ever desirous and desirable by being " in love ". If we love her, we hope that no swerve of hers will become an excursion and we value her resistance to temptation, but only in the theatre is it supposed that an engagement ring changes her physical nature and that because she loves one man the rest of the male species becomes instantly null, void and of no effect. But the conventionalists of the theatre will be troubled in any case, because Karen, though unmarried, is not without sexual experience. The English are a strange race. In life they recognize, permit and even enjoy great variety among those whom they love and admire, but in the theatre, where they sit in mass, they assume more than their fair share of the intolerance and hysteria of masses. This is particularly true of them in their sexual judgments. In the theatre, they divide women into two classes : " the good " and " the bad " ; they " put all their money on matrimony or the mantelpiece ". Even odder is their fixed idea that they must not accept, in a play, a woman's claim to be deeply in love and honour her for it, unless she is : (*a*) virgin, (*b*) married to a man they dislike and contemplating adultery with a hero of whom they approve, or (*c*) a *dame aux camélias*. Karen is protected by none of these categories. She is a woman of passion and integrity, not virgin, not an adulteress and not a courtesan, who now loves. By the mass-rule of pit and stalls, this is impossible, and yet almost every woman knows, in her own heart and often in her own experience, that it is not.

Karen is, then, what women are when their love is valuable to men—neither cowardly, prudish nor promiscuously licentious. She says openly what has, I

think, not been said in the theatre for over a hundred
years and not by an honourable character since the
Elizabethans—that she desires men ; and by this she
means not that she is undiscriminating or self-indulgent
—for evidently she is neither—but that the experience
of sex is, in her case, what Nature intended it to be and
what in women not aversionists it is—a delight, and not
an act of self-sacrifice. For saying this she will be reviled,
but it seemed to me necessary, after watching more than
two thousand plays, that so simple, and, outside the
theatre, so unrevolutionary a truth about women should
be re-stated on the stage. It was certainly necessary to
re-state it of Karen. That she is a passionate woman
with power to control her impulses is her distinction
from Lady Helston and the reason for her belief that she
can work with Ferrers without destroying him. If she
had been a cold or indifferent woman, this would have
been impossible, for she would then have done what
indifferent women invariably do—she would have held
herself out as a tantalizing prize and have used her
feminine allurements as a means of capture and of power.
In an age when women kept their own apartments, down-
stairs and up, and were, or were not, visited by men in
" hours of ease ", it was tolerable that they should be,
like Lady Helston, " uncertain, coy and hard to please ",
but nowadays, when they work with men, coyness is
a dangerous trick, and those women are most to be
honoured who have a singleness of mind that they also
wish to preserve and who feel and admit an equality of
desire. For where there is equality of desire, there is, in
restraint, a like equality and a mutual honour. It is

because she admits this equality and honestly makes the difficult experiment of working, in singleness of mind, with the man she loves that Karen is to be thought of as a woman of integrity ; and it is by putting a pinch of incense on the altar of Caesar, when Ferrers will not, that she proves herself to be what great and unembittered women will always remain—not more unscrupulous than men or more hesitant to die for their faith if necessary, but less rigidly bound by their prides to go to a stake that may be avoided. She and Ferrers have, as lovers, this in common : they do not surround the experience of sex with reasonless taboos or regard it as guilty in itself because there is pleasure in it ; they perceive, nevertheless, that, until promiscuity has robbed it of meaning, it expresses one of life's principal values, and so—because all values are inter-related—cannot be isolated or without consequence.

This is an attitude of mind less familiar in the theatre than in contemporary life, and whatever in the theatre is unfamiliar is dangerous. With this theme, a novel would have been safer. But I love the theatre. Since I was a midshipman in the China Seas, I have been fascinated by its glittering, sordid and enchanted craft. I should not die happy if I had not once attempted to write for it. An artist should learn to draw before he ventures to distort, and whoever wishes to experiment in the theatre must first recognize its present conditions, and accept their discipline, even while striving by a little to change them. He must understand that the writing of a speculative play has, to-day, much in common with the solving of a jig-saw puzzle or, to put the same notion more solemnly, with the composition of a sonnet. By the substitution of one word, I make Wordsworth my advocate :

> . . . to me,
> In sundry moods, 'twas pastime to be bound
> Within the stage's scanty plot of ground,
> Pleased if some souls (for such there needs must be)
> Who have felt the weight of too much liberty,
> Should find brief solace there as I have found.

The pages that follow express a group of ideas from which the play was an offshoot. Whom the play entertains may neglect the essay ; who cares for the essay may neglect the play ; but if there be one—and " such there needs must be ", as Wordsworth so cheerfully said—who, without deciding which is text and which sermon, receives play and essay into his own perspective, he will be a reader after my own heart.

August, 1938.

ON SINGLENESS OF MIND

All night the fury of contending will
Raged in my head,
Until my bed
Seemed the tormented world that devils fill
With anguish mixt and hungry violence.
I waited for the day with muted sense,
Too dry to weep, even my terrors dumb,
As if, while body waked, spirit were numb.

At last, as though I lay upon a hill
Above a valley choked by envenomed thorn,
Trackless and dark,
I saw a spark
Strike down from heav'n, whence a stream was born
Which, flowing from the zenith to the sea,
Fierce and unswerving as the zeal of saints,
Had yet the saints' reserved tranquillity,
And gave to earth, its genius unconfined,
The soundless passion of a single mind.

THE STREAM : *Verses on Singleness of Mind,
written among the Black Mountains*

ON SINGLENESS OF MIND

I

BECAUSE the history of man is a history of his spirit, *Its place in history* certain periods are thought of in terms of the idea, or group of ideas, by which they seem, in retrospect, to have been chiefly influenced. We speak of the Renaissance, or the Reformation, or the Struggle for Liberty—a practice that has the disadvantage of all headlines, but has been found convenient by historians of repute. It may, then, be permissible to suggest that the next hundred years will appear to future historians either as a period of disintegration and collapse or as one in which mankind conspicuously renewed its long and often interrupted search for singleness of mind.

Those who most aggressively call themselves "modern" and are so occupied in trimming their sails to each gust of opinion that they have no eye for changes in the weather will mock this prediction. They will say that the world, being plunged in economic and political confusion, must be chiefly concerned to discover and to apply political and economic remedies; that this, as Russia and Germany prove, is a period of mass-action; and that singleness of mind, like liberty, is part of an individualism discarded by "advanced" thinkers and to be, in the end, abandoned by all. They fail to discern that Communism and Nazi-ism, whatever their merits or demerits, had their origin in the singlemindedness of one man, and are, at least in theory, expressions of the supposed mystical unity, in the first instance, of a class, and, in the second, of the German race. Both these experiments may be considered a perversion of the idea of singleness, as the French Revolution was a perversion of the idea of liberty, for singleness of mind is the product of an inward choice of values, as they, in their political aspects, are not ; but they are experiments which, if regarded with detachment, show, as even the worst excesses of the Terror showed a hundred and fifty years ago, what impulse is thrusting forward the mind of the world. Those who still believe that economic materialism is the root of human destiny applaud or condemn only what is mediocre in the Russian and the German systems— their desperate palliatives, their insistence on dogma, their barbarous persecutions—and seldom recognize that what Germany and Russia have in common and what gives genuine modernity to their theories is the desire, felt in the marrow of contemporary civilization, to establish, amid the ruins of ambition to which the world has come, certain areas of mental absolutism. Mental absolutism—the power to assimilate and have repose in an idea—is one of the conditions precedent to singleness of mind.

One who thinks of himself as an imaginative writer first and last may be content to say no more than this on the political aspect of his theme. The duty of an artist in any medium is not to persuade men to action but to draw into the open ideas that may already powerfully exist in the shadowy places of the human consciousness, and perhaps to throw light upon the nature of these ideas and the nature of things : in brief, to impregnate the imagination of those by whom his work is received. My purpose is to recall from the shadow and to re-examine an ideal that has always been present in man's aspiration, not only as a retreat, a means of defence against confusion and evil, but, in another aspect, as an instrument of happiness and power.

None can say to what end man was brought into this world nor what the destiny of the race may be, yet there are great spirits who live not for their present ease but in quest of an impersonal end, as though a runner should spend himself in a relay-race for an unknown, and by him unattainable, prize. Leonardo was such a man, and who gives life for her child is such a woman. The distinction is not of talent but of spiritual genius and racial faith. The humblest may have it, the giants of power and intellect be without it. It is not definable in any person, for it is not a private possession ; its nature is to be continuous, like the handing on of a torch. Its convenient name is the Spirit of Man and the proof of its existence that, under this name, all men recognize it. *An instrument of the Spirit of Man*

There are recurrent periods of history in which it seems that the long struggle must end in defeat, the torch be dropped and mankind relapse into barbarism. Such a period followed the collapse of Roman power but ended in the Renaissance ; in such a period we live now who, if we hope for a renaissance, must look for it in a different kind. Our folly is not greater than our forefathers' but the instruments of our folly are more destructive ; our civilization is equipped for suicide as theirs was not, and stands in instant peril. The terror is not that men will die or that they will die uselessly and in misery, for men are replaceable; we attach overmuch importance to the preservation of our lives, which, in the reckoning of nature, are of small account. The terror is that a sonnet of Shakespeare may be lost as the poems of Sappho have been; or the cathedral at Chartres be destroyed; or the science of mathematics, the art of mathematics, be driven back to a cutting of notches on sticks.

This is the meaning of "relapse into barbarism"—an abdication of spiritual powers, a surrender of unique emblems—but even this is not the death of the Spirit of Man. A soul is not dead when it ceases to love but when it loses the capacity for love, and man is not lost, however barbarous, while there remains in him the power to wonder, and to feel his way, however blindly, towards a predestined fulfilment. To safeguard and renew this power is the supreme purpose of existence so far as our knowledge and intuition instruct us. We can do no more; the rest must be added unto us; if it is not, life has no meaning but appetite, and we are beasts deceived. We can do no more, in the Christian phrase, than seek God, that, finding him, we may at last know him, whom we do not know, and discover the nature of that invincible imagination which drives mankind towards an end that has borrowed his name.

Many are persuaded by despair that against the violence of the modern world there is no remedy but to escape or to destroy; but there is another within the reach of all—of a woman at her cradle, of a man of

6

science at his instruments, of a seaman at his wheel or a ploughman at his furrow, of young and old when they love and when they worship—the remedy of a single mind, active, passionate and steadfast, which has upheld the spirit of man through many tyrannies and shall uphold it still. This singleness of mind, called by Jesus purity of heart, the genius of love, of science and of faith, resembles, in the confused landscape of experience, a flashing stream, " fierce and unswerving as the zeal of saints ", to which the few who see it commit themselves absolutely. They are called " fanatics ", and indeed they are not easily patient of those who would turn them aside ; but, amid the confusions of policy, the adventure of being man and woman is continued in them.

II

The word " absolute " must continually recur, for, *Conditions precedent : absolutism* except through absolutism, singleness of mind is not to be understood. Because life is conditional and insecure and because no unhappiness is greater than that of division or entanglement, men have always sought for, and often have invented, absolutes to which they might cling. " I accept absolutely, and doubt no more ", has been the comfort of a thousand faiths. " I accord absolutely and recall myself no more " is the ideal of marriage. " I obey absolutely, and dispute no more" is at once the surrender and the joy of discipline. " I am God's absolutely and my own no more " is the mystical end of saintliness.

Absolutism, false or true, has a dramatic quality that produces, upon those who encounter it, a violent effect of attraction or hostility. Few are indifferent to it. One may be indifferent to the devoted competence of Bertrand but not to the absolute ambition, at once genius and madness, of Bonaparte ; or one may disregard a tolerable and discreet virtue, but must either passionately follow John the Baptist or demand his head upon a charger. It is not the virtue or the wickedness but the absolutism of supremely great men that rouses mediocrity to persecute them ; it is genius that is sent to the cross, for taxpayers feel that the policeman can protect them from Barabbas ; and absolutism is, for this reason, perilous in a world with a habit of compromise, the more perilous because the barren and false is not easily to be distinguished from the fruitful. Men of blood claim it and are worshipped by their followers. The arrogance of a mind locked in error may have the appearance of absolutism and draw to it other minds less resolute. The perversity of it is spiritual pride and what the clear intellect of France contemptuously describes as *enthousiasme*—a buzz of the emotions that forbids reason to be heard. In this, and in all its corrupt forms, it has the characteristic of having been reached by seizure in a mood of fear, whereas true absolutism seems always to have been approached by a series of reasoned acceptances, the passion that inspires it being an impersonal one.

A girl of my acquaintance, a Catholic by birth, was unhappy in her home and wished to be a nun. Though not a fool, she had a habit, of which she was aware but unable to cure herself, of speaking foolishly ; her words, she felt, betrayed her. She sought admission to a silent order but was refused. The refusal surprised and wounded her, for she was persuaded of her vocation and could not understand by what she was disqualified. She waited, asked again for admission, and was again refused. After an interval, she asked a third time, and was at last told why she was unacceptable. She sought the veil as an escape from a life in which she was unhappy ; she had chosen a silent order because she was ashamed of her own tongue ; she had a negative vocation, and a positive vocation was necessary. She must desire silence as a means to the glory of contemplation and must enter the cloister believing she had been summoned thither to serve God in this, and in no other, way. Her instructress drew a faultless distinction between a perfect and an imperfect absolutism.

The power of what is absolute to fascinate men consists not only in its contrast with their haphazard existence but in their sense of its being immune to human frailty. When I was at Oxford, I stayed during part of a Long Vacation with a friend whose father was a country vicar. He was an old man, a scholar, and to me almost a stranger. For these reasons, and not because he was a priest, I asked him to give me advice on a subject that was troubling me and that concerned, as well as myself, people unknown to him. He was remote from my confusion and I valued his detachment. In his library, when we were seated opposite each other, he told me to begin my story. I asked that what I had to say should never be told again ; he agreed, pledging his word, and I began to describe my difficulty to him. After a sentence, he interrupted me, went to a corner of the room, and returned, wearing a stole. " I gave you my word," he said,

" and have no reason to believe that I should not have kept it. But I am a talkative man, I am married. This "—he touched the stole—" makes secrecy absolute." I have long forgotten his advice, but I recall to-day the pang of happiness, the sense of release, almost of redemption, which sprang from my encounter, at a moment when the world seemed to be foundering under me, with a promise that could not be betrayed. I believed then, and believe now, that by his act this man had, within the area of his pledge, exempted himself from human frailty. Nothing could have deflected him from secrecy ; he would have died rather than speak. My joy was not that my secret was safe, for I had not doubted its safety, but that here, suddenly, within my own experience, was a thing decided, unchangeable, final—an area of absolutism, small indeed, but perfect. I had not been ignorant of the confessional rule, but do not young men hear of love before they experience it ? This was my first experience of an inviolable secrecy. I felt as a seaman might who, drifting on to a lee shore, casts an anchor that holds.

Conditions precedent : concentration

A second element in singleness of mind is a power to concentrate. Concentration may be acquired. Professors of the subject, to prove its difficulty, challenge us to perform the " elementary exercise " of confining our attention to the door-knob for a period of sixty seconds. We fail, for the exercise is not elementary. No one is naturally interested in door-knobs ; there is nothing in them to engage the mind. A man must discover his own elementary exercise within the range of his natural interest, aiding himself by such devices as rhymes or

mnemonics continually repeated, by a physical and re-
petitive movement which he is able to make while his
mind is directed elsewhere, by breathing exercises, or by
any one of a thousand rhythmical processes. It is for this
reason that a child forms a habit of low, monotonous
chanting, or of touching railings as he passes them. He
is not thinking of the chant or of the railings. He is
using them as excluding agents, that his mind, given
wholly to the subject that fascinates him, may be safe
from invaders.

Though concentration is not itself a spiritual state and
the attainment of it is a disciplinary and mechanical process, it is necessary to singleness of mind, and we do well
to beware how we laugh at or interrupt the attempts,
often superficially ridiculous, of those who struggle for
it. Many of the peculiarities of childhood—the sudden
and unaccountable retreats of a child naturally sociable—
spring from an intuitive desire to exercise this concen-
trative self-discipline and to enjoy the solitary and
receptive bliss that is its reward. The demands made
upon a child's attention by men and by nature itself
become more than he can endure. He is asked to learn
French from nine to ten, Latin from ten to eleven, and
to pursue other studies at all hours of the day. His games
are organized and made competitive ; he is expected to
treat them as a part of ambition. Whatever his mind
touches—the life of animals, the power of engines, the
movement of the skies, the dimly perceived relationship
between men and women, the innumerable magics of
words, of music, of signs and emblems, of God—recedes
at his touch and he must follow it, breathless. Enthusiasm

B

breaks upon him, then another, and he forgets the first, as he forgets a toy in mid-floor ; he is blamed, and blames himself, for having forgotten. A month ago, his rabbits were his life ; he fed and watered them, visited and had a secret understanding with them, for they were more than rabbits—a part of his kingdom, aspects of himself. To-day they are a burden he has accepted and from which, it seems, he will never escape. You are an hour late in feeding your rabbits. What are you doing there, lying on the floor ? Reading. What is the book ? You are only pretending to read. You can't understand a word of it. And it is almost true. There are many words he cannot understand. But what is the difference between reading and pretending to read ? The name, *Paradise Lost*, fascinated him ; the unutterable prestige of Milton —the fact that he was not to be understood like the Caldecott—drew him on ; the verse was an incantation that made a giant of him, for the Garden was a part of his kingdom, and the sounds, the incomprehensible thunders, were proceeding from within himself. What are rabbits ? The garden-boy can feed them.

Later, in a class-room, the galley-slave of ink, he struggles by all the normal processes that have been taught him, the elimination of brackets, the laborious discovery of roots, the preliminary quest of y, to bring x to earth. No doubt it will come, but the way is long, there is a fly against the window-pane, a shadow of chestnut leaves on the black-board, and the lid of his desk, beneath encrustations of ink, is grained—a soft grain in which one can drive channels with a pencil. The elimination of brackets is a tricky business ; plus and minus perilously interchange ; he must keep his mind upon it, thrusting on for x, as though it were the premiership or a crow's nest or the city of Trebizond ; but a city is a town that contains a cathedral—is there a cathedral at Trebizond ? There is no royal road to x ; the rough work must be done in the margin, its result brought over ; step by step this impersonal and deadly x must be pursued until—suddenly there is a click of the brain, like the shutter of a camera, and x is his own, a part of himself, as mysteriously unrecognizable as the sound of his own voice, but his own, a rhyme, a peal of bells in his head : Four point one one ! Four point one one ! Please, sir, is the answer : Four point one one ? You have been very quick. Show me. The book goes up. Where are the steps ? What's the good of guessing ? It's the steps that matter, not the result. But come here. What *is* this ? How did you guess ?

There is no answer and can be none. The rabbits and Milton and Four-point-one-one are all, it seems, parts of himself—and who is he ? The boy who buries his head in the scrum ? Or the terror by night that his father may die ? Or the creature who, while he writes an essay, modestly circumspect, in hope of a red alpha, is hit by a flight of words as he was by that arrowy x, and throws alpha to the winds ? What will become of him, who is thus wildly at sixes and sevens, while others seemingly are steadily content ? You should not worry so much. You should not ask : What will become of *me* ? You should learn, my boy, to think more of others and less of yourself, and to take life as it comes. You should cultivate a sense of humour.

13

But life comes fast, a shower of arrows, and death faster.   It is not old men who fear death.   To a boy it strikes in every clock and burns in every bonfire of autumn.

> But at my back I always hear
> Time's wingèd chariot hurrying near.

You are wasting time.   When will you learn to concentrate ?   Smith minor has reached Exercise XXXVII.

> When I behold, upon the night's starr'd face
> Huge cloudy symbols of a high romance,
> And think that I may never live to trace
> Their shadows . . .

then, under the lash of time, in the hail of perception, the child rushes hither and thither.   Pity him when he comes to rest.   Do not probe his hiding place.   He lies awake, telling stories to himself ; do not reprove him, do not measure his candle.   There is a long ridge of stones above the orchard ; each day, without stumbling, without dislodging a pebble, he must traverse and retraverse it seven times.   Permit imagination its ritual ; grant the eye its focus.   At all costs he must be alone, idle, still.   What are you doing ?   Nothing.   Have you taken any exercise to-day ?   No.   Leave him.   Have mercy on him.

> Weave a circle round him thrice,
> And close your eyes with holy dread,
> For he on honey-dew hath fed,
> And drunk the milk of Paradise.

At this moment in his writing of *Kubla Khan*, Coleridge

" was unfortunately called out by a person on business from Porlock, and detained by him above an hour ".

Though a man have a nature capable of absolutism, *Conditions precedent: acceptances* without which he is a ship that has no anchor ; and though he have skill to concentrate, which, in the same metaphor, is a navigator's skill ; he is yet far distant from singleness until by acceptances he has freed himself for the voyage.

To accept an evil is not the same with being resigned to it. To accept is to see and see through it, to penetrate and so to become independent of it. To be resigned is a closing of the eyes, an abdication of spiritual energy, a blind submissiveness, a slavish walking in the shadow of an evil ; but acceptance a making of it translucent, so that, though it continue, it has no power of darkness, and the saying of Jesus, " Resist not evil ", is emptied of its paradox.

Of forces opposed to singleness of mind, some are part of common experience and may be called general impediments, and some, peculiar to this man or that, are particular impediments. These last are as various as the expressions of the human face, and their power seems often freakish and unaccountable. One man is prevented from singleness, and his mind continuously disturbed, by knowledge of a physical defect which is, in fact, scarcely an inconvenience to him and of no account with the world ; thus Byron by his lameness. Another is unable to free himself of the memory of a past failure ; a third is irrationally bound to a dead passion ; a fourth cannot escape from superstitions that have long ago been discounted by his intelligence. I have known a woman, naturally tranquil and independent, whose mind was thrown into turmoil by the life of modern cities. They provoked in her an emotion equivalent to the hatred that springs from a vendetta—an emotion, that is to say, from which no present remedy could free her and which her reason was unable to transcend. Another woman, not personally known to me, whose life was devoted to bringing up children of the very poor and who, for their sakes, had taken upon herself poverty, chastity and other great denials, was tormented by an extraordinary desire to travel. In her later years, she was described as being of a habit so peaceful and ardent that one might have supposed her acceptance to have been long complete and her singleness made perfect ; but it was not so ; this desire had remained in her powerful and recurrent, presenting itself in all the forms of a major temptation, racking her with self-pity, urging her to rebel against her own rule, reminding her that to travel was in itself innocent, suggesting to her that her life's work was valueless, even that it was a form of self-glorification, and that she would do well to abandon it. Bound to England by her work, she had had strength to resist each onslaught of this desire, but for many years had been unable to prevent its being an impediment to her singleness of mind. The remedy she had discovered was as strange as the desire itself. Whenever the longing to travel came upon her, and unknown rivers and mountains and cities would not be banished from her thoughts and dreams, by a single act of acceptance she converted prospect into retrospect, and said : " I have come home from a long journey ", and went among her children that day in the mood of one who had been long absent, seeing them afresh, loving them afresh, perceiving them with new, unstaled recognitions. By this means she reached a point at which the desire for travel ceased to be an enemy of her singleness of mind and became contributory to it. She hung on the wall of her room a great map of the world that, in the body, she would never explore.

Such particular impediments and their remedial acceptances do not contribute easily to a discussion of principle ; they are too various and depend too much upon private circumstances ; little can be deduced from them except that, in each case, acceptance appears to consist rather in passing through an impediment than in resisting an assault. Is this true of the general impediments to singleness of mind—for example, carnal desire and the fear of war ? Are these also to be overcome by the method of acceptance ? If so, what, in each case, does acceptance mean ?

I differ from many of my contemporaries in believing *Carnal acceptance* that the sexual act is an act of consequence, and, at the same time, that it is not in itself evil. It is an act of consequence in this sense : that, unlike other pleasures of the body, it has, among civilized men, powerful and unavoidable associations distinct from the pleasure it gives. We know, and cannot by any callousness escape our knowledge, that it is a means by which love is expressed and life perpetuated. A materialist cannot make it, even for himself, a purely carnal act ; though his companion be an anonymous harlot, he is unable to cancel her humanity, making of her no more than a cup from which he drinks, nor can their act be other than an imitation or perversion of another greater than itself. There are materialists who claim that they are able to break down or " forget " the non-sensual associations of the act of sex, and on this basis they justify promiscuity. To them there are two answers : first, that the " forgetting " is never complete ; second, that the struggle to " forget " is a struggle to annihilate the natural extensions of the act and so a reduction of the forgetter's personality, a deliberate sacrifice of his wholeness and integrity, a form of imaginative abuse. Among us, we being what we are and inheriting from the past the ideas we do inherit, it is inescapably true that the experience of sex is associative as other sensual acts are not. It cannot be isolated as a pleasure of the body. It is an act of consequence for good or for evil.

But it is not in its nature evil, nor is the pleasure that it gives to be discountenanced. It is to be avoided for two reasons only—if it does harm to others or if it stands between a man and a spiritual development of which he would, in a state of chastity, be capable—and neither of these conditions is inherent in the act itself. The face of the world would be changed if this were understood and if the experience of sex were considered to be innocent unless its circumstances made it guilty. There are millions who believe that they understand and recognize this, but they do not. They say that they are " tolerant ", and, in that very word, contradict their claim to understanding. The idea of sexual enjoyment is so closely associated in men's minds with the idea of sin that the effect of this association is felt in every department of life. Even when marriage has permitted, and, indeed, required the act, it is never acknowledged, never plainly spoken of, as it would be if it were not felt to be disgraceful. A man will say that he dined with his wife but not that he lay with her. Why? Is the act ugly? As the means by which children are procreated, is it not declared by the Church to be the first cause for which matrimony was ordained? Is it not lawful? Is it not " true ", " honest ", " just ", and " lovely " ? Why, then, unless the physical love, even of man and wife, is considered to be still not " pure ", is it not " of good report " ? Yet men and women will not speak of it to others and will seldom name it between themselves. In music-halls it lies at the root of a furtive humour that is the psychological equivalent of fear and is called " daring " because it is ashamed. Outside the language of medicine or the slang of whores, there is no verb except " to lie with ", that describes the act without an overtone of sin or brutality, and " to lie with " is left by modern taste to the obscurity of the Bible. The latest revisers of the Prayer Book have done their utmost to expunge, or to make indirectly allusive, every direct reference to the act of sex that occurs in the Marriage Service.

The consequences of this idea that the act is evil in itself and cannot, even by marriage, be freed of its association with sin are socially and morally disastrous, for there is madness in the belief that the act by which we live, by which love is expressed and the race continued, is an act of shame. There are contradictions that man cannot entertain without disturbance of his mind's composure, and this is one of them. It is responsible for the hysterical relish of a great section of the public for sexual crime and sexual scandal. It converts them, and their press through them, into torturers of men and women. It leads judges, whose duty is to administer the law and be done, to torment with fierce moral lectures, that are no part of their judicial privilege, persons whom a jury has acquitted. To the public disgrace, it drives from public life men of the quality of Parnell. It is a cause of subterfuge in lovers and of spiritual pride in those who would persecute them. It is especially dangerous when the sexual act has, in truth, been made by circumstances either a crime or a sin, for then this false conception of the act itself lays upon sexual wrong-doing so great an emphasis that it is no longer seen in the perspective of justice or of the Gospels; the wrong-doer is denied the pity that is felt even for murderers, he is ridiculed and spat upon, his suffering is turned to jest, and priests revile him as if the sins of the flesh were greater than the sins of the spirit. They deny their master, for this was not the teaching of Christ.

It was not his teaching that the act of sex is in itself disgraceful. In reproving adultery, he reproved, not the act of sex, but a breach of the spiritual and contractual bond of marriage, his context (Mark x. 11, Matt. v. 32, Matt. xix. 9) being the laws governing divorce. He makes it clear (Matt. v. 28) that the act in breach of contract is not, in his view, more blameworthy than the lust to commit it, the whole tenor of his thought seeming to be that the desires of the flesh ought not to be allowed to interrupt spiritual singleness but that the acts of the flesh, even where sinful, are to be received not with " tolerance ", nor with the anger he directed against spiritual pride and the desire for applause, nor even with aloof pity, but with compassion. " He that is without sin among you, let him first cast a stone at her. . . . Woman, where are those thine accusers ? hath no man condemned thee ? She said, No man, Lord. And Jesus said unto her, Neither do I condemn thee : go, and sin no more " (John viii. 7-11).

I can find nowhere in the Gospels a general upholding of the ascetic rule by Jesus. He likened his own followers, as Dr. Gore pointed out, to " the children of the bride-chamber round about the bridegroom ", and there is in Matthew xix. 11 and 12 an elaborate passage of the utmost significance as a pendant to the ruling he has just given on divorce. His disciples, in question of his ruling, say : " If the case of the man be so with his wife, it is not good to marry ", and Jesus answers : " All men cannot receive this saying, save they to whom it is given. For there are some eunuchs from their mother's womb ; and there are some eunuchs which were made eunuchs of men : and there be eunuchs which have made themselves eunuchs for the kingdom of heaven's sake. He that is able to receive it, let him receive it." Upon this the authoritative Anglican comment of Dr. Goudge and Mr. Levertoff is : " Celibacy is a loftier condition than marriage in the Lord's eyes "—a comment which is hedged a little elsewhere and cannot easily be justified in the text. Jesus says that there are some who by nature or by the act of others or by their own act have been rid of sexual capacity, and that to these a rule applies not applicable to other men. He expresses here no approval of celibacy and no criticism of marriage. The passage is vital because upon it rests the argument that it is my purpose to combat : that celibacy is good in itself, apart from special circumstances which may require it, for, if this were true, it would follow that the act of sex must be bad in itself, apart from special circumstances which may make it so. This is not the teaching of Jesus, who cared above all else, not for the observances or renouncements of the body, but to create and to preserve spiritual singleness.

Dr. Gore, formerly Bishop of Oxford, wrote : " It was not asceticism, as generally understood, which was proclaimed by our Lord. . . . He never depreciated marriage or the body". And later, having spoken of the " remarkable capacity " of religious Jews to allow respectable sins, Dr. Gore added : " Nothing is more startling than our Lord's absolute refusal to recognize this distinction of respectable from disreputable sins. Certainly fornication or theft or violence is not worse in His eyes than avarice, unmercifulness, contempt, hypocrisy, selfishness, ambition. It is not that He palliates sensual sin. His words where He speaks of it are penetrating and severe. But He seems to regard it, and the like disreputable sins, as less hardening than respectable sins. ' The publicans and the harlots go into the kingdom of heaven before you.' " This, though it occurs in the same volume with the comment of Goudge and Levertoff on Matthew xix., is no exaltation of celibacy or condemnation of the act of sex in itself. It is the comment of a great scholar and a saintly man. Yet even Dr. Gore used the word " startling ". Why was he " startled " by the refusal of Jesus to distinguish between respectable and disreputable sins unless there lingered, even in his mind, traces of that obsession which vitiates, and deprives of perspective and compassion, contemporary judgment of the acts of sex?

Celibacy " for the kingdom of heaven's sake " is justly credited among the supreme renouncements. The great professions, even in their differences, honour one another—the priest the seaman, the seaman the doctor, the doctor the priest—for all these are driven by an impersonal passion which is a bond between them. They understand absolutism wherever they find it, though its form and rule are not their own. They know suffering, and obedience, and the death of self-will that is beyond obedience, as men that have no training cannot know them. A discipline chosen by masters of the spiritual life is not scorned except by upstarts and fools.

But the splendour of celibacy is a desperate splendour ; its denials are wounds ; to support it without spiritual pride requires a genius of humility ; and the method of acceptance is an alternative to it, less in the degree of bodily suffering but harder in the sense that it is not imposed from without by a great tradition but must be discovered by each man for himself and within himself. It rests upon two things : a will to preserve singleness of mind from destruction by bodily desire, and a recognition that the act of sex is an act of consequence but not of itself evil. If it were not an act of consequence, it would be possible to argue, with the promiscuous, that desire may be eliminated by satisfactions. If it were of itself evil, there would be no alternative to renouncement of it. Acceptance is neither promiscuous nor ascetic. On particular occasions and for indefinite periods, which

23

may be spoken of as periods of separation or absence, it cuts off the current of sexual power, using to this end, if it be necessary, the ascetic discipline of fasting and other quietings of the body ; but these are dangerous in themselves, they recall the mind to the subject it would avoid ; and acceptance is an ordering of the imagination within the body as it is, not a killing or changing of the body. A writer at a crisis of his work, a priest at grips with his faith, a man of science at the height of his problem, may see before him a time in which his singleness of mind can be safeguarded only by renouncement of the act of sex ; he enters then deliberately into a period of separation ; but his renouncement is not the final renouncement of a celibate, and a time comes in which he accepts the act without attachment to it. The test of non-attachment to a thing is a power to value it, to convert it while present to the purpose of singleness, and to forgo it at any time without an agony of denial. A man must learn to quit a woman as a seaman his country, remembering her beauty without hunger, returning to it without enslavement, and this he teaches himself to do not by rejection of her, but by devotion to his voyage. It is the miracle of singleness that the love of it draws all nature and wisdom into its service ; it enables the acceptances by which it is preserved ; by the power of its own light it throws back the shadows that threaten it. The freedoms of the spirit are not attained by violence of the will but by an infinite patience of the imagination.

Acceptance in war   Some will find it harder to apply the principle of acceptance to the impediment of war than to the impediment of sex, for they will say that to fight is evil and vain and contrary to nature, as the act of sex is not. Those who interpret literally the doctrine of non-resistance and declare that in no circumstances will they fight, may be likened to celibates and be honoured for their will to absolutism as celibates are, but their rule is open to the same criticism and admits of the same alternative. Here the alternative may, perhaps, be stated without arrogance in the form of a confession of personal faith.

I wish to live in such a way that at last I may be able to say truly that there is nothing except a pen and my own room that I cannot do without. These, and what may proceed from them, are my singleness of mind ; the worst that peace or war can do to me is to destroy that room ; the worst I can do is to betray it. I believe that death cannot destroy it ; I know that by dying I shall not betray it ; therefore, the idea of death is, in me, at worst, the idea of sadness at parting, not a motive to live. This room is my self, my integrity ; from it proceeds what value I may have to my God and to my neighbour ; the worth of my experience is that little by little it teaches me how to carry this room with me wherever I go and how to inhabit it. Every man has his own room. I submit that his first duty, by which all others are to be judged, is to protect it, for nowhere else can he serve men or see God. It is his purity of heart, his genius, the place of his receiving the spirit of man and of his giving it again. If war comes, and his service is demanded, shall he refuse or obey ? Shall he by non-resistance to the enemy resist Caesar, or, obeying Caesar and rendering to him what is his, pursue, even in this, the method of acceptance ? I do not seek to persuade others. Each is the defender of his own room. If any believe that, refusing to fight, he can yet preserve his integrity from political bitterness and spiritual pride, let him choose his way as the celibates choose theirs. But there is another way that may be followed by men to whom war is vanity. They may leave their pen on their table for a little while and carry their peace through an invisible battle.

III

Its nature and enemies

Singleness of mind is a form of genius, but it is not what the world commonly means by genius—an extreme of talent and skill ; for it may be possessed by those who are never masters of their fellows, though a few look to them, seeing in what way they are masters of themselves.

In humble men it may be surer than in the princes of intellect, who feel the horse of genius quiver under them and are impatient to be away. For the sake of their science or their art they will, indeed, exclude all else, and for its sake will suffer or die, but when they see victory before them in a near battle and are denied it by the slowness of men, their pride swings to arrogance, which is converted to despair ; in their anger they mistake the battle for the campaign, and lose all, even their singleness of mind. Simple men, who walk through life on their own feet, unless a passing angel lift them a mile on their way, and who have no fiery horse under them, are not in peril of being thrown ; they are steadfaster in the acceptances they have made.

Sometimes, when a young man lies down at night, it

seems to him that his day has been mis-spent, though he has done harm to none and performed his tasks and obeyed the law. Or a girl says : Why am I here ? Who needs me ? I grow old. Or a soldier, seeing the battle, sees also mankind divided against itself and says, as Prince Arjoon said : " Woe is me ! what a great crime are we prepared to commit, that for the lust of dominion we stand here ready to murder the kindred of our own blood ! I would rather patiently suffer that the sons of Dhreetarashtra, with their weapons in their hands, should come upon me, and, unopposed, kill me unguarded in the field." Or the young man, tired of his plough or his ledger, will wish to take up arms to punish tyrants and redeem the world by his energies now seemingly wasted, or the girl make herself a parasite on the civilization that she cannot serve. There is no end to divisions of mind, and no will that can make a pattern of them, and no escape except they be passed through.

Every obsession is an attempt to escape. There are groups of men who can think only in terms of their own political creed, who pride themselves that they and they only are facing reality, and will admit nothing to their judgment—neither art nor science nor religion—unless it plead in the language of their economics. Those who differ from them they call " escapists ", without guessing that economic obsession is their own bolt-hole. Afraid to ask what a man is and what he may become, they ask what he has and what he may obtain, as if their standard of possessions were indeed a " standard of life ". But life is more than they will allow, and it is from life itself they are escaping. Self-confinement within an idea, used as protection against the impact of other ideas, has superficially some of the appearances of singleness of mind, but is a perversion of it.

Singleness itself has certain clearly recognizable characteristics. Like obsession or singleness of idea, it has a centre of devotion—for example, Newton's devotion to the group of ideas expressed in his *Principia* —but, unlike obsession, it is flexible ; it does not treat reasoned criticism as a heresy but as a stimulus, and it does not prevent a man from continuing in peace though his circumstances change, as Newton's did when he went to the Mint. It appears also to endow those who possess it with Goethe's extraordinary power of harnessing the outer and fully conscious mind to the collection of material for the subconscious mind, so that a single-minded man, however simple his life or unspectacular his behaviour, slowly produces upon his associates an impression that he is inspired—or, to avoid a word that begets controversy—that his subconscious mind is continuously nourished and impregnated from sources not at once apparent to them or to him. Finding this to be so, he may say, simply, that God provides for him, or he may use another form of words with which to describe the renewals within himself : the effect is the same—that he is renewed, and, in his face, the youth of another world looks out from the age of this.

This renewal, and the long struggle for it, and the contradictions of aspiration and conduct which are the wounds of that struggle, have made him at all times a target for men who shun the solitudes of the mind. To them his failures are hypocrisy, his advances arrogance ;

his separation from their custom is an offence. Every age has its own weapon against genius and singleness of mind. Ours is the cult of uniformity. Class by class, men are included by a hedge of prescribed opinion ; so, perhaps, they were always ; but in the past to break it down was to rebel and carried with it the penalties and honours of rebellion ; to-day it is an act of petty indecency at which all good citizens laugh behind their hands. Uniformity has become so great and so insidious a persecution that the peril of genius is not so much that it may be sneered at as that it may learn to sneer at itself ; for the inquisitor who seeks now to crush singleness of mind is not orthodoxy, to which there has always been a straight answer, but that acidity of derision and self-derision which is miscalled " a sense of humour ".

The Squire of Cilmery has a gift of plain questioning that opens the heart. Once he asked an old ploughman what he should do if he owned the squire's rents. Summat useful, the man said ; then, after thought : a bit o' ploughin', may be : the answer not of dull content but of an art loved singly, not to be forsaken, its own reward, as though to the same question Irving had returned : I should act.

Bunyan in his *Grace Abounding* tells of his examination by Justice Keelin :

" Then, said he, hear your judgment. You must be had back again to prison, and there lie for three months following ; and at three months' end, if you do not submit to go to church to hear Divine service, and leave your preaching, you must be banished the realm : and if, after such a day as shall be appointed you to be gone, you shall be found in this

29

realm, etc., or be found to come over again without special license from the King, etc., you must stretch by the neck for it, I tell you plainly ; and so he bid my jailer have me away. I told him, as to this matter, I was at a point with him ; for if I was out of prison to-day I would preach the gospel again to-morrow by the help of God."

At this distance in time, Bunyan does not appear laughable, but who doubts that he appeared so then to Justice Keelin, Justice Chester, Justice Blundale, Justice Beecher and Justice Snagg ? Their names declare them English, and to the English all extremists are absurd ; even the ploughman's story is never told without a smile, though he was harmless enough ; if he had been danger-ous, an active genius, a disturber of established com-promise, he would have been laughed to scorn ; and it must be understood by whoever loves singleness of mind that " a sense of humour " is his enemy—an enemy in modern England so adroit, so powerful, so artful in retreat, so brilliantly subtle in the very stupidities of its attack, that it must be faced.

Its strength is that it intends no evil. Those who most elaborately cultivate it are unaware that it is a vice, and, indeed, suppose it to be a virtue. In their view, it is a means of preserving a desirable mental balance, a refusal of extravagant emotion, a wise choice of understatement and the middle way. It is, as it were, a sheep-dog trained to bark cheerfully in drawing-rooms or on battlefields at the first sign of original virtue. We are to work as a " team " ; we are to speak proudly of the national gift for compromise ; we are to insist that our artists behave well in polite society and that our preachers prefer what

Luther called " the epistle of straw " to the Sermon on the Mount. " Blessed are the pure in heart, for they shall see God," said Jesus. He had no gift of denigration, no joy in derision, no " sense of humour ". Shakespeare had none. Wit and mirth he had, but not the sense of humour that is for ever blunting the edge of spiritual truth. He who wrote the Sonnets, or Hamlet's bidding to Ophelia, or *Troilus and Cressida*, or Cleopatra's scene with Mardian had no moderation, no smell of the sixth form, no sense of humour. Milton had none ; Wordsworth none ; Shelley none ; Nelson none. Consider Nelson. The modern English have transformed and rewritten him, have made of him an idol in their own image, as they have made an idol of Shaw, that he may be tamed and they comforted. But Nelson, their hero, was not tame ; it was Byron who played cricket for Harrow and survived. Nelson was never tame or conformable ; he won battles by a method of his own, flourished his mistress in the world's and in his wife's face, quartered himself on her husband, insisted upon wearing all his decorations at Trafalgar, and kissed his Flag-Captain—a piece of emotionalism so alarming in a national hero that English gentlemen with a sense of humour are still hoping that what he said was " Kismet, Hardy ". But the hard truth is that Nelson was a highly sensitive, self-dramatizing egoist with three saving qualities : that he had a single-minded, and therefore creative, belief that God's breath was in his sails ; that he substituted genius for pedestrian talent ; and that he had no sense of humour to sap his faith. It was his good fortune to spring from the eighteenth century.

To-day we should scarcely have permitted such a man to command the Fleet, for the sense of humour by which we are now ruled avoids emotion and vision and grandeur of spirit as a weavil avoids the sun. It has banished tragedy from our theatre, eloquence from our debates, glory from our years of peace, splendour from our wars ; it has so mocked, at opposite extremes, the spirit of Milton and the spirit of Keats that to be a puritan or to be a romantic is accounted equally absurd and there are no heroes but in celluloid. One by one, it has damped the sparks of life—art, love, duty, faith—until the Bible has begun to vanish from our language, and Romeo himself speaks to Juliet as if he were a dumb-waiter offering her an ice. It is talent's sneer at genius, in whatever form genius appear. It is mediocrity's hatred of the Spirit of Man, a blanket on vision, a yelp at saints.

But the Spirit of Man is indestructible and singleness of mind is its instrument. Krishna gave his answer to the prince whose conscience would not allow him to go into battle. " Resolve to fight. . . . Let the motive be in the deed, and not in the event. Be not one whose motive for action is the hope of reward. Let not thy life be spent in inaction. Depend upon application, perform thy duty, abandon all thoughts of the consequence, and make the event equal, whether it terminate in good or evil. . . . The wisdom of that man is established who in all things is without affection (attachments). . . . His wisdom is confirmed when, like the tortoise, he can draw in all his members and restrain them from their wonted purpose. . . . A man of a governable mind, enjoying the objects of his senses, with all his faculties rendered obedient to his will, and freed from pride and malice, obtaineth happiness. In this happiness is born to him an exemption from all his troubles ; and his mind being thus at ease, wisdom presently floweth to him from all sides."

For, like all great ends, singleness of mind is not an end but a beginning. It is a receptive state, the converse of hardness of heart. It is the womb of reason. A countryman has it who, being himself very old and without hope of the event, goes upon his knees to plant an acorn in the ground.

THE FLASHING STREAM

CAST

The play was first performed at the Lyric Theatre, London under the direction of Mr. Godfrey Tearle, on Thursday, September 1st 1938, with the following cast, here given in the order of their appearance :

COMMANDER HENRY CARR, R.N. . .	Mr. Leo Genn
DENHAM (Corporal of Marines) . .	Mr. Roger Maxwell
LIEUT.-COMMANDER PETER BRISSING, R.N.	Mr. Anthony Ireland,
COMMANDER EDWARD FERRERS, R.N. .	Mr. Godfrey Tearle
LIEUT. - COMMANDER RICHARD SAND-FORD, R.N.	Mr. Laurier Lister
LADY HELSTON	. Miss Marda Vanne
REAR-ADMIRAL SIR GEORGE HELSTON, Bart., C.B., R.N.	Mr. H. G. Stoker
THE RIGHT HON. WALTER HARROWBY, P.C., M.P.	Mr. Felix Aylmer
KAREN SELBY	. Miss Margaret Rawlings
CAPTAIN WINTER, D.S.C., R.N. . .	. Mr. Desmond Roberts

Time : The Present

Scene : The living-room of the officers attached to Commander Ferrers' experimental unit in the British island of St. Hilary, in the Atlantic

Act I   *Scene* 1 : An evening, early March
                     2 : After dinner, the same evening

Act II   *Scene* 1 : The morning of July 15
                     2 : August 16. 5 P.M.

Act III   Mid-October

      Producer   .   .   .   .   .   Mr. Peter Creswell

A few changes of detail, to be made during the last days of rehearsal, may not have been incorporated in the present text.

ACT I

ACT I

*The Block House, formerly a fortress, on high ground
three miles from Kendrickstown, in the British island of St.
Hilary, in the Atlantic. It is now used as a naval experimental station.*

*The scene is a big, plain whitewashed room furnished as
a naval mess. It is the general living-room of the officers
attached to* COMMANDER EDWARD FERRERS' *experimental
unit. Beyond it, up stage, there is to be seen through a wide
arch, which may be closed by heavy doors now open, a
verandah with a couple of small tables and some chairs. Sky
beyond and indication of flowering shrubs. The verandah
is approached from within the room by a few shallow steps,
and whoever leaves the verandah for the open air goes down
steps to the garden level. The verandah is, in effect, a
platform at the back of the stage. On the audience's right,
down stage, a settee and a small table for drinks behind it.
Above these a door opening on a passage which leads to the
mess-room, ante-room and other rooms of the Block House.
Below and above this door, two drawing-office desks with
electric light attachments and high stools. On the left, up
stage, seen through a wide arch, a short flight of steps leads
first to the Control Room door ; then, out of sight, to the
room in which* FERRERS *sleeps. The door of the Control
Room is like the door of a huge safe. In the archway, there*

*is a piano.   A table, L.C., running up and down stage, is
covered with a table-cloth of service pattern.   Other tables
and chairs.   The upholstery is of leather.   There are maps,
charts and a few pictures.*

*It is a clear evening of early March, warmer than in
England.   Before dinner.   Daylight lately gone.*

COMMANDER CARR, *in mess dress, enters through the
arch L.   He is about 47, solid, kindly, able ; never openly
emotional ; the balance and common sense of a brilliant
group of men.*

CARR

(*Shouting through open door*)

Ferrers !

FERRERS

(*Off*)

What ?

CARR

Where did you leave it ?

FERRERS

On the piano.   (*As* CARR *picks up cigarette-case,*
DENHAM, *corporal of marines, enters, puts newspapers in
order on side-table and tidies up the room.   CARR begins to
play the piano and breaks off.*)

CARR

Denham, when you've got things straight in here, take
this to Commander Ferrers.   He's upstairs dressing.

DENHAM

Very good, sir.

CARR

And you might report progress.   We don't want him late for his guests.

DENHAM

I'll give him a jog, sir.

CARR

Which means ?

DENHAM

Tell him his watch is slow, sir.

CARR

(*Smiling*)

He's pretty close on the mark.   You won't catch him that way.

DENHAM

I'm not saying he'd swallow it, sir.   But it do give people a turn to say their watch is slow.   May think you're a liar, but they can't be that sure.   It's like winkin' the eye about a man's girl.   She may be an angel with knobs on, but it makes him look slippy.

CARR

Go easy, Denham.   He's on edge.   He's done two men's work since Mr. Selby was killed.   Go easy.

DENHAM

Very good, sir.   (*Makes for door.*)

CARR

Find out if you can how he wants people seated at

to-night's dinner. I suppose he'll have the Admiral's lady on his right and Miss Selby on his left. Find out where he wants the First Lord and the Admiral. The rest of us can arrange ourselves. The Flag-Captain too. Where's he to go ? Ask that if you can. But use your judgment, Denham. Don't worry him for orders. He doesn't like invasions of this place—particularly female.

DENHAM

Some of us could do with a bit more of it, sir.

CARR

More what ?

DENHAM

Skirt, sir.

CARR

I dare say. But that isn't his view. As long as the experiments go on, the fewer people get their noses into this Block House the better—men or women.

DENHAM

It's more than a year now, sir. It comes a bit hard on the married men.

CARR

It does. I'd have brought my own wife out if there'd been a chance of it, but there's only one house in Kendrickstown that hasn't fallen to pieces, and the Admiral's wife has that. Anyhow, Denham, what about the single men ?

DENHAM

It's harder on the married, sir.

CARR

Is it ?

DENHAM

What I say is : if it's not, it ought to be.

CARR

Are you a puritan, Denham ? Is that usual in the Marines ?

DENHAM

Begging pardon, sir, it's very usual in the Marines. (*Then seeing that his leg has been pulled*) Well, sir, you're married yourself. It's not for me to be telling you. I only hope some of the hands'll stick it. They're weak—sailors. (CARR *begins to play piano ; then as the significance of* DENHAM'S *remark strikes him, he stops.*)

CARR

Did you say " stick it ", Denham ?

DENHAM

I did, sir.

CARR

What, exactly, did you mean by that ? Is there trouble ?

DENHAM

Oh, I'm not suggesting mutiny, sir. Nothing of the

43   D

kind. Commander Ferrers, he only has to look in on 'em when they're in the workshops and make one of his jokes straightfaced without batting an eyelid and they'll sit here in this sweaty island till he tells 'em to quit. But it's easier for us up at H.Q. than it is for them.

CARR

I wonder. Hadn't struck me. In some ways I suppose it is.

DENHAM

Well, I had a brother in the war, sir. Corporal he was at the time. South Wales Borderers. He wasn't never one of them clever ones that went about saying the staff was shirkers. Regular soldier he was, long service and a good 'un. But he always said: "The Staff knows what's going on. That makes it interesting for them. But we don't. Sitting in trenches," he said, "is like sitting at the pictures when you can't see the screen." And it's the same with the men in the workshops, sir.

CARR

But they know what we're driving at.

DENHAM

They do and they don't, sir. They know that what they're making is a kind of aerial torpedo. They call them Scorpions, same as us, but——

CARR

If the Scorpions work, no bomber can live in the air. Isn't that something?

DENHAM

That's what I keep telling 'em, sir. But some people want to know everything—specially the engineering kind. You and the Commander and Mr. Sandford and Mr. Brissing, you send down designs for separate parts, and they make 'em blind and they make 'em accurate, but they can't piece 'em together. More than a year of that. It takes some sticking.

CARR

But they must work blind, Denham. No one outside can have the complete plan. Too much hangs on it.

DENHAM

I know, sir. But it's not knowing how long it will last. If I could write and say: "Dear Mother. Home by Christmas" it'd be easier. I'm not complaining, sir. If the Scorpions is going to mean no enemy can touch us by air, all right. But the last trial didn't come to much, except that Mr. Selby was killed.

CARR

Wasn't meant to. It was preliminary.

DENHAM
(*A little too familiar*)
When's the next to be, sir?

CARR

When we're ready. (*This is a snub and* DENHAM *is silent.* CARR *leaves piano. Goes to a drawer from which*

45

he takes material for letter-writing and lays it out on table.)
Are Mr. Selby's things all packed up ?

DENHAM

Yes, sir.

CARR

Ready to be shipped home ?   Nothing left out ?

DENHAM

Commander Ferrers went through 'em himself, sir.

CARR

I see.   (CARR *is unscrewing and testing his fountain pen.*)

DENHAM

With Mr. Selby dead, sir, and the work slowed down, perhaps the Admiralty would be sending out someone to help the Commander ?

CARR

Mathematicians of the Ferrers and Selby rank don't grow on raspberry bushes, Denham.   There aren't twenty in the world—and they have jobs, and most of them aren't English.

DENHAM

I see that, sir, but——

CARR

There's no but about it.   Here we are and here we stay until the thing succeeds—or fails.

46

FERRERS
(*Off*)

Carr, where the hell are those cigarettes ?

CARR

Take them.

DENHAM
(*To* FERRERS)

Coming, sir. (*Exit* L. CARR *sits down at table and begins to write letter. Enter* LIEUTENANT-COMMANDER BRISSING, R. *He is in dress-shirt, trousers, wellingtons, braces—no tie. Young, handsome, a little vain, potentially a lady-killer, but that is not his profession. A* "*star*" *Gunnery Officer, he has first-rate intellect.*)

BRISSING

Where's Denham ?

CARR
(*Steadily continuing his letter*)

Gone up to Ferrers.

BRISSING

He put me out lightning-conductors. Why are we in mess-dress ?

CARR

Because, my boy, the First Lord of the Admiralty is dining to-night.

BRISSING

Even so——

CARR

And because the Admiral's wife thought she'd like our legs to look pretty.

BRISSING

Ferrers' legs.

CARR

May be.

BRISSING

How that woman loves to give orders !

CARR

May be.

BRISSING

I can't find my tie.

CARR

It's in the loop of your shirt.

BRISSING

Where ?

CARR

Hanging down your back.

BRISSING

Damn ! (*Finds it*) One of the disadvantages of a celibate life is that there are no mirrors. What are you doing ?

CARR

Writing a letter home.

BRISSING

You won't get far with it this evening.

CARR

I shall when they've gone. I write a kind of serial letter. A bit at any odd time. Then put them together when there's an outgoing mail.

BRISSING

I scribble mine at the last moment.

CARR

The other way keeps you in touch. It's more like talking. Something comes into your head and down it goes. My wife does the same.

BRISSING
(*Enviously*)

You must feel *safe* !

CARR

She permits me that illusion. Is Sandford dressed ?

BRISSING

Out of his bath. . . . Things seem to have happened since we went away.

49

CARR

You and Sandford gave things time to happen. Nineteen hours over leave.

BRISSING

I know.   Completely genuine breakdown.

CARR

Have you reported ?

BRISSING

Couldn't until we had got into uniform.   Ferrers said much ?

CARR

About you ?   Very little.   Bit awkward that neither of you was here for the First Lord's inspection this morning, but Ferrers and I took him round.   Last night was the trouble.

BRISSING

Why ?

CARR

Someone from here had to go down into Kendrickstown and call at the Admiral's house as soon as the First Lord had landed from his liner and settled in.

BRISSING

Wasn't that up to Ferrers himself ?

CARR

He wouldn't go.

BRISSING

But why ?

CARR

Just wouldn't. (*Abandons letter*) You know, Brissing, he's devilish on edge. Sounds mad, but, in some odd way, he goes on looking for Selby.

BRISSING

Did you gather they were as close friends as that, when Selby was alive ?

CARR

I didn't—not fully. And it's not all personal. Mathematics means more to Ferrers than anything on earth. It's his language. It was Selby's too and it's not ours. What they cared about wasn't the Scorpion itself but the maths of the thing. That's the point. Without Selby he's alone in a foreign country.

BRISSING

Even so, I don't see why he couldn't pay a duty call at the Admiral's house.

CARR

Because Selby's sister is there.

BRISSING

And the Admiral's wife. She'll have her knife into him if he doesn't play his cards. Ask me, he's a fool to avoid her.

CARR

But he's never looked at her.

BRISSING

Precisely. Why d'you think she patronizes Sandford? She doesn't care a damn for *him*. Trouble is, Sandford himself is badly hit, but he'll get over it. Meanwhile, she's dangerous to Ferrers. She sees him here, shut up, working like hell, concentrated on his job. That fascinates some women. It's odd. They want to break up a man's work because it keeps them out, and they want to be—the inspiration of it. That's her ladyship's trouble. Any man who's running a show is fair game to her. If she was in a train, she'd try to seduce the guard. If she lived in Rome, she'd pester the Pope. And when she got no change, she'd hate them. Ferrers is precisely the kind to drive her mad. If he had a bit of sense, he'd play down to that woman.

CARR

By which you mean—go to bed with her?

BRISSING

You have the simple mind of a happily married man, Carr. No—on the whole—not. He'd have to get out again. Then there *would* be hell to pay. But he might at least go through the polite motions of thwarted longing. (*Enter* DENHAM, L.)

CARR

All right?

DENHAM

Coming down, sir.

BRISSING

I'd better get dressed before he comes.   (*Exit*, R.)

CARR

What about the seating at dinner ?   Where are the ladies to go ?

DENHAM

I asked him, sir.

CARR

Well ?

DENHAM

He said I was to give you the message in his own words, sir.

CARR

Well, go on.

DENHAM

He said : " Tell Commander Carr that he can put the women where the——"

CARR

All right, Denham.   Carry on now.

DENHAM

Here he is, sir. (*Enter* FERRERS.   *He is dark, keen, very alive.   In his walk, the buoyancy of a single-minded*

*man with natural authority ; in his abrupt manner the im-
patience of one who knows that the minds of others move
slower than his own. To fools, he is arrogant, but not in
face of his own job. His imagination can leap to other
people's point of view ; when it does, it endows him with rare
sympathy and tenderness.* CARR *sits down again to his
letter.*)

FERRERS

(*Holding out wrist to* DENHAM)
Look at that.   (*Pointing to clock*) And that.

DENHAM

Yes, sir.

FERRERS

Well, look at it.   You can't see it from here.

DENHAM

(*Walks to clock, turns, stands at attention*)
Yes, sir.

FERRERS

Well ?

DENHAM

I'm sorry, sir.   But it did the trick, sir.

FERRERS

It did.   Time for a gin before they come. One pink,
one orange, Denham.

DENHAM

Very good, sir.

FERRERS

Tell the sentry to report at once when he hears the Admiral's car on the lower road.

DENHAM

Very good, sir. (*Exit.*)

FERRERS
(*To* CARR)
I wish you hadn't let us in for this.

CARR

I couldn't help it. Admiral's orders. (*He finally abandons letter and carries writing material to the drawer from which it came.*)

FERRERS

He can't have ordered himself to dinner in our mess.

CARR

He made it pretty clear. It's the First Lord's idea, I think.

FERRERS

Harrowby. He's an odd cove. I like politicians when they have brains. . . . But the women?

CARR

That's Harrowby's idea, too. After all, you've got to see the Selby girl some time.

FERRERS

I suppose so.

CARR

Her brother may have been a civilian, but she probably thinks of you as his commanding officer. There'll be things she'll want to ask.

FERRERS

I don't want to go over and over it. Selby's dead. All our work's held up without him. I can't say : " That's the desk your brother worked at. That's the settee he sat on to drink gin. He died happy, talking of you."

CARR

It happens to be true.

FERRERS

What ?

CARR

That he died talking of her.

FERRERS

He died talking of calculation-groups forty-three to eight. Group 46 was on his mind. There's something new to come out of that. I can't get——

CARR

May be. But he talked of her too.

FERRERS

Apropos of Group 46. He said she'd know. He always said she was a finer mathematician than he was himself. . . . My God, what a waste ! Why I let him of all men go up as an observer——

CARR

My dear Ferrers, he asked for the job. You have no need to blame yourself.

FERRERS

Haven't I ? I let him go. . . . What have you been packing away in there ? Not work ?

CARR

Only a letter. (DENHAM *comes in with drinks and goes out again.*)

FERRERS

What's the girl's name ?

CARR

What ? Selby.

FERRERS

I mean the other.

CARR

Karen.

FERRERS

I remember. Karen Selby. Well, here's to her. (*Drinks.*) She's a mathematician anyway. (*Enter* BRIS-SING *and* SANDFORD. *The following passage up to*

DENHAM'S *entry is strictly Service.* SANDFORD *is quieter than* BRISSING, *but of a steadier and even deeper intelligence. He is a romantic where* BRISSING *is a realist. Towards women a little too doglike.*)

FERRERS

Why didn't you report?

SANDFORD

We weren't in uniform, sir.

FERRERS

Well, this isn't the uniform to report in.

SANDFORD

There wasn't time for a double change. I'm sorry, sir.

FERRERS

What happened?

BRISSING

My mare went lame just after we had started for home. I had to wait with her while Sandford went for another mount.

SANDFORD

It took me eight hours, sir. I lost my way. When I found him, my own horse was all in. Anyhow it was dark. We had to camp again and come on at sunrise.

FERRERS

All right. Can't be helped. (*Enter* DENHAM *with tray, decanter, gin, etc.*) You'd better get your drink in

before the women come.   After that you'll have to talk.
. . . Brissing, you're the poodle-faker in this mess.
When the car is reported, go out and meet them.   They'll
like that.

BRISSING

I'll tell the sentry.

FERRERS

That's done. . . . (*To* SANDFORD) Dick, your job is
to keep Lady Helston in a good temper.   Is that con-
genial ?

SANDFORD

I'll try.

CARR

It may not be easy.   As far as I could gather, the
Selby girl isn't a joy to her.

BRISSING

Another woman wouldn't be.

SANDFORD
(*Defensive*)

Well, if you had a perfectly good blue-stocking thrust
on you as a guest——

BRISSING

Why " thrust " ?   Anyhow where else was the girl
to go ?

SANDFORD
(*To* BRISSING, *angrily*)

I dare say there is nowhere else.   That doesn't make
it easier for Lady Helston.   That's why I said " thrust ".

CARR

It's more or less true, I'm afraid. She was in the same liner with the First Lord. He took her under his wing to the Admiral's house.

SANDFORD

With the result that Sybil Helston——

BRISSING

Sybil Helston! Damn it, you worry that woman's name as if it were a bone. (*To* FERRERS) Mr. President, sir, can we have a round of drinks off anyone who repeats a lady's name more than three times a minute? (*Enter* DENHAM.)

DENHAM

Sentry reports car approaching, sir.

FERRERS

On you go, Brissing.

CARR

Bring them in by the verandah. (*Exit* BRISSING.)

SANDFORD

Why that way?

CARR

Avoid the smell of cooking.

SANDFORD
(*Laughing*)
Bless you, sir.   You're the sanity of this place.

FERRERS
(*Who is walking up and down in a state of extreme
nervousness*)
Why in God's name can't women leave you alone ?

CARR
It's not the girl's fault.   She didn't know Selby was
dead when she sailed.   Harrowby told her on board—
from his own wireless.   Be gentle with her, Ferrers.
. . . If you can't, be gentle with yourself.

FERRERS
You saw her last night ?

CARR
Yes.

FERRERS
Speak to her ?

CARR
A bit.

FERRERS
What's her line ?

CARR
Didn't say much.

61

FERRERS

About Selby, I mean.

CARR

Asked where he was buried.   I told her.   She said :
" Why didn't you bury him at sea ? "

FERRERS
(*Interested*)

Did she ?

SANDFORD

Bit odd for a girl.

FERRERS

What ?

SANDFORD

To think of that.

FERRERS

Why odd ?

SANDFORD

Lady Helston has a horror of burials at sea.   She says
it's so lonely.

FERRERS

Burials are.   What's the point of dying, if you can't
be alone even then ? (*Enter from verandah* MR. HAR-
ROWBY, *First Lord of the Admiralty, dry, thin, deliberate,
silky—with a twinkle ;* REAR-ADMIRAL SIR GEORGE
HELSTON, BART., *a good seaman but unimaginative, easily
flattered because he is weak and full of vague good-will and*

62

likes to be liked ; LADY HELSTON, *much younger than her husband, at once bright and intense. She is well-bred, well-dressed, affected, but no fool.* FERRERS, CARR *and* SAND-FORD *go forward to meet their guests. Greetings.*)

LADY HELSTON
(*To* FERRERS)

What a lovely room this is ! (*To* ADMIRAL) George, isn't it a lovely room ?

ADMIRAL

Well, my dear, you're the expert on interior decoration.

LADY HELSTON

It's not that. It's the atmosphere of it !

SANDFORD

We find it a bit monastic.

LADY HELSTON

That's why it's such a perfect background for a party.

SANDFORD
(*Ingratiating*)

I have mixed you your own cocktail.

LADY HELSTON
(*Snubbing him*)

Dick, that's sweet of you, but may I have sherry ? (*To* FIRST LORD, *who is talking to* FERRERS) We owe it to you, Mr. Harrowby, that we're asked here at all. Commander Ferrers never gives a party if he can help it.   Do you, Edward ?

FIRST LORD

Well, you mustn't expect the prior of a monastery to invite temptation into it.

LADY HELSTON

Not even with whitewash as a background ?   I always wear a dress with flame in it and trust to Edward's imagination to supply a forked tail.

FERRERS

Where are our other guests ?

LADY HELSTON
(*To* ADMIRAL, *irritably*)
Where *is* that girl ?

ADMIRAL

Winter's following with her in his car.

LADY HELSTON

I know that.   But they ought to be here by now. They started just behind us.

FIRST LORD
(*Now alone with* FERRERS)
She may disturb the monastery a little.

FERRERS

Who ?

FIRST LORD

Miss Selby.

FERRERS

(*Sharply*)

Why do you say that ?

FIRST LORD

The more because in her case the disturbance will not be deliberate.   She doesn't need flame in her dress.   Are you a judge of women, Ferrers ?

FERRERS

Not by profession, sir.

FIRST LORD

Good.   But I hope an observant amateur ?   It is, I think, important.

LADY HELSTON

(*Cutting in*)

What is important ?

FIRST LORD

To have a good memory, Lady Helston.   I was trying to recall those lines of Pope's :

" I know a thing that's most uncommon,
      Envy be silent and attend.
   I know a reasonable woman,
      Handsome and witty but a friend.

   Not warped . . ."

Do you remember, Ferrers ?

FERRERS

I'm afraid not, sir.

FIRST LORD

Perhaps we shall be reminded before the evening is out.

BRISSING

(*In verandah*)

This way.   Shall I lead on ?   (*But he stands aside and* KAREN SELBY *enters, followed by* FLAG CAPTAIN *and* BRISSING.   CAPTAIN WINTER *is prim, efficient, hard, shifty.* KAREN *is dark and not conventionally pretty.   Her power is in her movement, her voice, the impact of her imagination and intelligence.   She is wearing an evening dress, beautifully made and of one flat colour—or, preferably, of black, for she is in mourning for her brother, and, if the actress likes black on a white background,* KAREN *brought a black dress on her voyage.*)

LADY HELSTON

Edward, you must do the introductions.   You haven't met Miss Selby.

FERRERS

(*Taking* KAREN'S *hand*)

No.   (*Greets* FLAG CAPTAIN.   *Then to* KAREN *again.*) Look, Brissing you've met.   He's the gunnery expert.

KAREN

I'm afraid we nearly ran him down.

66

FERRERS

You saw Carr yesterday evening. That leaves Sandford. Dick, come and be introduced. (SANDFORD *is handing sherry to* LADY HELSTON. *Now he comes to* KAREN.)

SANDFORD

How d'you do. I have to apologize.

KAREN

For what ?

SANDFORD

Five minutes ago I decided you were a perfectly good blue-stocking.

FIRST LORD

I can assure you she's neither.

KAREN

Neither ?

FIRST LORD

A blue-stocking—nor perfectly good.

KAREN

(*With a shade of serious emphasis*)
That's true.

FIRST LORD

This is an officer I haven't met. You are a torpedo-man, Mr. Sandford ?

SANDFORD

Yes, sir. Brissing and I (*he draws* BRISSING *in*) were away fishing. His mare went lame.

FIRST LORD

Any fish ?

FLAG CAPTAIN

If there were, they'd have gone off in this weather.
(*They drift away, talking of fish.* DENHAM *supplies every-one with drinks.* ADMIRAL, FIRST LORD, SANDFORD, BRISSING *are in one group.* CARR *is talking to* LADY HELSTON.)

KAREN
(*To* FERRERS)

You are Edward Ferrers.

FERRERS

I am.

KAREN

My brother always wrote of you by both names.
That's why I used them.   I think of you that way.

FERRERS

I see.

KAREN

He loved you.   You know that ?

FERRERS
(*Cold but trembling*)

We were good friends.

KAREN

I'm sorry.   You hate to talk of him.

68

FERRERS

I'm sorry for your sake, Miss Selby. I ought to have said so. Coming out here— (*He abandons polite condolence*) It's my work takes me back.

KAREN

Group 46 ?

FERRERS
(*Suspicious*)
What do you know of Group 46 ?

KAREN

You needn't worry. He didn't give away any secrets. All I know is part of the mathematical process —nothing of what it's leading to. It was in Robin's last letter.

FERRERS

I see. Do you make anything of it ?

KAREN

Yes.

FERRERS

How great a mathematician are you ?

KAREN

I——

FERRERS

No. You can answer that to me. Selby said you came before him. Is that true ?

69

KAREN

Yes.

FERRERS

Well, thank God you can say it.   Do you always tell the truth ?

KAREN

About mathematics.   (*There is a pause, neither can speak.*   FERRERS *goes to table where drinks are.*)

CARR

Still there are *things* you can believe in—if not people.   Aren't there ?

LADY HELSTON
(*Bored*)

There may be.

CARR

More sherry ?

LADY HELSTON

Dickie mixed me my own cocktail.   Can I have that ?

CARR

Of course.   (FERRERS *returns towards* KAREN.   *On the way, meets* CARR.)

CARR
(*To* FERRERS)

Which is her ladyship's cocktail ?

70

FERRERS

She's drinking sherry.

CARR

She's mixing them.   (FERRERS *reaches* KAREN.)

FERRERS

You have nothing to drink.

KAREN
(*Looking into his face*)
He never sent a photograph.   I've never seen one.

FERRERS

Of what ?

KAREN
Of—any of you.   (*She turns her head away suddenly*.)
I think I *should* like a drink.   (BRISSING *has come down
with* ADMIRAL *and* FIRST LORD *and is within earshot.*)

BRISSING
I'll get you one.   (*Goes to table.*)

FIRST LORD
Ferrers, have we a minute before dinner ?

FERRERS
It's overdue, sir.

71

FIRST LORD

Never mind.   I'd like a word.   (*He draws* FERRERS *aside.*)

ADMIRAL

This is your first experience of a naval mess, Miss Selby.

KAREN

I went to a dance in a Yugo-Slav warship at Corfu.

ADMIRAL

They have a drink called Šljivovica.   It's a kind of plum-brandy.   (*The dinner bugle sounds.*)   You don't recognize the dinner bugle.
(*Sings*)   " Officers' wives have puddings and pies,
Sailors' wives have skilly."

LADY HELSTON

George, in a moment you'll be teaching Miss Selby knots and splices.

ADMIRAL

I should like that.

KAREN

So should I.

CARR

(*Detaching* KAREN *from them*)
Are you a painter, too, Miss Selby ?

KAREN

A painter ?   No.   Why ?

72

CARR

Only that your brother was. He and I went out sketching together. That's one of his things over there. I'll take it down for you.

KAREN

No, don't do that. (*They go over* L.)

LADY HELSTON

George, I want you to do something for me.

ADMIRAL

What, again?

LADY HELSTON

Now don't be crusty. It makes you seem older than you are. This is quite simple.

ADMIRAL

As long as it's not a Service matter. I've been wanting to say for some time, my dear, that on Service matters you really must leave me to myself.

LADY HELSTON

Don't you value advice?

ADMIRAL

Of course I do. Of course I do, between ourselves. But you must be more discreet. People will begin to say——

LADY HELSTON

This isn't a Service matter. It's personal. Don't

73

you think, after dinner, Commander Ferrers might show us his Control Room ?

ADMIRAL

Show you, you mean ?

LADY HELSTON

He never has.   He always avoids and hedges.   Perhaps he thinks you wouldn't approve.   If you issued an order——

ADMIRAL

But, my dear, this is a dinner-party.   An order——

LADY HELSTON

Don't be stupid.   If you say you approve, that will be enough.

ADMIRAL

Better leave Ferrers alone.

LADY HELSTON

But you don't disapprove ?

ADMIRAL

N-no.

LADY HELSTON

That's all I want.   (*Enter* DENHAM.)

DENHAM

Dinner is served, sir.

ADMIRAL

(*Glancing round and seeing that* FERRERS *is occupied with* FIRST LORD)

Shall we lead on, Ferrers ?

FERRERS

Please, sir.   (*General drift towards door* R.)

FIRST LORD

Don't think I'm trying to force your hand, Ferrers.

FERRERS

What you suggest can't be done, sir.

FIRST LORD

Possibly not.   But can anything else be done ?   Who else is there ?

FERRERS

Aren't there any men in the world ?

FIRST LORD

Not here. Not with her qualifications. You see, Ferrers, I'm getting old. Women, so to speak, don't hang out flags for me—white or red—though sometimes I get a glimpse through a window in passing. The things that chiefly interest me are (*a*) cats, (*b*) the safety of Great Britain.   And whether it's a man or a woman sells me the cat I want—or the peace of the world— makes no odds to me, as long as I get it. You are younger.

FERRERS

The thing won't work, sir.

FIRST LORD

Young enough to be afraid of women—or of your-self. . . . I believe Mr. Sandford spoke of the lady as " a perfectly good blue-stocking ". I presume he hadn't seen her.

FERRERS

I have. However good she is at her job, she can't work in this unit.

FIRST LORD

You dislike her ?

FERRERS

That's not the point, sir. I——

FIRST LORD

Never mind. Never mind, then. We must not spoil our dinner. (*The others are all in the mess-room. The* FIRST LORD *and* FERRERS *move to the door. On the way the* FIRST LORD *stops. His bantering tone is gone.*) Is it true, Ferrers, that Miss Selby is among the first six mathematicians in the world ?

FERRERS

I'm not good at team-making, sir. Can you tell me who are the first six poets in the world ?

FIRST LORD

My question was, I admit, a crude one. Still, you can answer it.

FERRERS

The answer is : roughly—yes.

FIRST LORD

The first six ?

FERRERS

Selby said her work in the astronomical observatory at Green Hill was beyond anything of his.

FIRST LORD

That is what I want you to consider while you eat your soup. (*They move on. He stops again.*) Imagine her in trousers, my dear Ferrers. In dealing with women, I have found it a useful exercise. God so made a woman that in trousers a part of her truth conspicuously appears.

FERRERS

Not unbecomingly.

FIRST LORD

No. . . . No. . . . But with a salutary candour.

Curtain

ACT I

Scene 2

The same, after dinner. The stage empty and almost dark. DENHAM *brings in coffee and liqueurs, puts them down and turns on the lights. The diners begin to enter from the mess-room. When they have disposed themselves, the* FIRST LORD, ADMIRAL *and* FLAG CAPTAIN *are at the piano, and remain there in conference, unheard except when, in the chance silence of the others, a sentence or two of theirs comes through. The* FLAG CAPTAIN *is sceptical and disapproving of what is being said to him.*

LADY HELSTON, KAREN, BRISSING and SANDFORD help themselves from the trays.

FERRERS takes CARR by the arm, brings him right down stage past the others and talks with him eagerly. CARR *is laughing good-humouredly.*

FERRERS
(Cutting him short)
Yes, I know. But he means it.

CARR
That she should come here ?

FERRERS
In Selby's place.

78

CARR

Who said politicians were without ideas ?

FERRERS

But seriously. You have your head screwed on—perhaps better than any of us.

CARR

At first glance, I like the girl.

FERRERS

As a girl ?

CARR

As a human being, too. She runs straight—and fast. (*Their talk continues.*)

LADY HELSTON
(*Taking a pace towards the group by the piano*)
Are we going to play, Captain Winter ?

FLAG CAPTAIN
(*An awkward courtier. Now a little vague, for he has been interrupted*)
Charming. Charming. . . . Bridge ? . . . Yes, I'd like a game presently.

LADY HELSTON
(*Mimicking*)
Charming. Charming. . . . Out on the verandah I think. (*To* BRISSING) Or will the cards blow away ?

79

BRISSING

There's not a breath.

LADY HELSTON
(*To* SANDFORD)

What are they up to, Dick ?

SANDFORD

Who ?

LADY HELSTON

Over there.   A conspiracy ?

SANDFORD

Harrowby is probably telling his best story.

LADY HELSTON
(*Going across again*)

Mr. Harrowby, is it true that all the wickedest stories come from the House ?

FIRST LORD

Not *from*, Lady Helston.   We keep them to ourselves.

LADY HELSTON

That's selfish.   Why ?

FIRST LORD

Because they're so often true.   (*Turns back.*)

LADY HELSTON
(*To* SANDFORD)

Now you try.

SANDFORD

What ?

LADY HELSTON

To break them up.

SANDFORD

Why should I ?

LADY HELSTON

They're scheming something. . . . Try.   You'll see.

SANDFORD
(*Glancing*)

Better leave them.

LADY HELSTON
(*Contemptuously*)

You may be right.

BRISSING

Are we quarrelling ?

LADY HELSTON

Not yet.

BRISSING

Then let's begin.

SANDFORD
(*Nettled*)

It has nothing to do with you—whether I do what
Lady Helston wants or not.

81

BRISSING

(*To* KAREN)

Getting a rise out of Dick Sandford is only a game, Miss Selby. In this place you take your entertainment where you find it. Brandy? (*There is a momentary silence as he pours it out.*)

FLAG CAPTAIN

I think you have too much confidence in him.

FIRST LORD

What do you say, Admiral?

ADMIRAL

I don't like it myself, sir. But I see no other way of getting the work done. I repeat I don't like it, but if your view is set, I don't oppose it. (LADY HELSTON *and* SANDFORD *are occupied with each other.*)

BRISSING

(*To* KAREN)

What are they talking about?

KAREN

Who? I didn't hear.

BRISSING

The First Lord and his cronies. . . . You're not hearing much this evening.

KAREN

I'm sorry.

BRISSING

Are you usually absent-minded ?

KAREN

No.

BRISSING

I thought not.

KAREN

Was I at dinner ?

BRISSING

Ferrers was on your other side at dinner.

KAREN

(*Deliberately flat*)

My brother had told me so much about him that——

BRISSING

Listen.   They'll drag you into bridge.

KAREN

They can't.   I don't play.

BRISSING

Good.   Then let's clear out of this.

KAREN

Clear out ?

BRISSING

Into the open. Walk down to the signal station.
The moon's up. I'll tell you why before you ask. I——

KAREN

You do believe in progress!

BRISSING
(*Looking at her*)

So do you.

KAREN

I see. But do you usually rush your fences quite
like——

BRISSING

No. But if I don't have you to myself now, it's ten
to one I never shall. I'm drunk of course. Anyhow
you think I am which comes to the same thing.

KAREN

No. I think you're in love. . . . Not with me. . . .
Is that true ?

BRISSING
(*Astonished by her intuition and grateful for it*)
Yes. Now you'll hate me.

KAREN

No. I never hate people in love. If I were in love
and he—hopelessly out of reach—anyhow I'm made that
way.

84

LADY HELSTON
(*Returning to them*)

Dick says we might make a four and leave the conspirators to conspire.

KAREN

I can't play.

LADY HELSTON

A mathematician who can't play bridge ! Edward can't lose.

KAREN

I'm sorry.

SANDFORD
(*Eagerly to* LADY HELSTON)

Come down to the signal station.

LADY HELSTON
(*To disappoint him, to* KAREN)

If you will come too ?

KAREN
(*To* BRISSING)

I should like to.

BRISSING
(*As* LADY HELSTON *and* SANDFORD *move up towards the verandah*)

No. Why the hell should you ?

85

KAREN
(*Smiling*)

Fate.

BRISSING

Or drink. . . . I'm sorry.

KAREN
(*Takes his arm*)

I like live animals.

BRISSING
(*Suddenly*)

Are *you* in love ?

KAREN
(*A short, astonished laugh*)

Give me time.

BRISSING

You asked *me* !

KAREN

I *told* you ! (LADY HELSTON *and* SANDFORD *are now in the verandah arch. The conference by the piano has broken up and the* FLAG CAPTAIN *intercepts her.*)

FLAG CAPTAIN

Now what about bridge ?

LADY HELSTON

Is the fate of nations sealed ?

FIRST LORD

Probably it is.

LADY HELSTON

Then let's play.

FIRST LORD

Not for me, I'm afraid, unless it's backgammon.
(KAREN *and* BRISSING *go out.*)

LADY HELSTON

You, Dick ?

SANDFORD
(*Hating it*)

I'm bad you know.

LADY HELSTON

I know you overbid. Never mind. It passes the
time. That's three. (*She turns to* FERRERS) What about
you ?

FERRERS

Carr will play.

CARR
(*Doing his duty pleasantly*)

Certainly. (*He begins to move up towards the
verandah.*)

FERRERS

Well, Carr, that's your last word ?

CARR

Yes. I see no other way.

FERRERS

I think you're mad.

LADY HELSTON
(*To* FERRERS)
What are you two so deep in ?

FERRERS
We were discussing whether men grow to resemble their dogs. (*The bridge-players go off to the verandah.*)

ADMIRAL
Ferrers, the First Lord has been telling me of the proposal he made to you before dinner. I gather you are against it ?

FIRST LORD
Oh come, Helston, that's a very leading question. Let us take it easy. (*The* ADMIRAL *and* FIRST LORD *sit, but* FERRERS *remains restless.*)

FERRERS
Have you spoken of it to Miss Selby ?

FIRST LORD
Certainly not.

FERRERS
Mustn't that be done ? What's the good of discussing whether we'll have her until we know whether she's willing to come ?

FIRST LORD
Or I might say, is it not perhaps indiscreet to ask a woman to change her whole way of life until we know whether you are willing to employ her ? . . . No,

Ferrers. This is a matter of choosing your own personnel. Not only that—but the member of your staff
who is to be your own closest associate. I issue no
orders.

ADMIRAL

Certainly, I don't.

FIRST LORD
(*To* FERRERS)
But I should like to understand your objections.

FERRERS

Among men—aren't they plain enough ?

FIRST LORD

Not if the men are doing a job that means anything.
Women have worked with men before.

FERRERS

This is a naval mess. Try bringing a girl to live in
a wardroom at sea.

ADMIRAL

But she wouldn't *live* here.

FERRERS

In effect she would, sir. We work to all hours. . . .
And this place is more cut off than any ship at sea. This
island stays put in the Atlantic. It doesn't go into
harbour and give leave.

89

FIRST LORD

Sandford said " monastic ". Does young Brissing treat it so ?

FERRERS

In fact he does—not without dust and heat. The local alternative isn't all it might be—and he's devoted to some girl in England. Carr is married. Sandford —(*he glances at* ADMIRAL *and hesitates*)—Sandford sticks to his job. I won't have them disturbed. I won't have myself disturbed. Besides, if she came, where *would* she live ?

ADMIRAL

That is a difficulty.

FIRST LORD

Is there no inn ?

ADMIRAL

There's a native inn. It is a house—that also supplies what Ferrers calls the local alternative.

FIRST LORD

Most unfortunate. No other quarters ?

ADMIRAL

None, except in my own house.

FIRST LORD

Would that be inconvenient ?

ADMIRAL

To me not at all. I should have to consult my wife.

FERRERS

(*Interrupting*)

None of that is the point.   If she comes at all, quarters shall be found.   (*To* FIRST LORD) You still don't understand, sir, what the difficulty is.

FIRST LORD

What is it, Ferrers ?

FERRERS

Have you any real notion of how this place is run ? We five—we four—live a very curious, specialized life.

FIRST LORD

In what sense ?

FERRERS

What do you think we have in common ?   We're all naval officers—that may be—Selby wasn't even that— but the Navy, as such, isn't what holds us here.   Carr's older ; when this is through he'll take a fourth stripe and retire ; but he's giving up here and now what is life to him—wife, sons growing up, a daughter he worships— the honest-to-God existence he loves—all on this gamble. Dick Sandford's the finest torpedo officer in the Service ; Brissing's gunnery isn't far behind ; they're young, desperately ambitious, and they're losing sea-time ; they're out of touch.   Here they live—no women, no leave, no company but their own, prisoners for all intents and purposes—all for an invention of mine.   The Government thinks it's wild-cat——

FIRST LORD

No.

FERRERS

Some do.

FIRST LORD

Not the Prime Minister.

FERRERS

Very well. . . . Isn't it true the Admiralty is impatient for results ?

ADMIRAL

That's not unreasonable. My wife's brother, Brian Wedgcroft, who's a member of the Board, feels, I know——

FIRST LORD

I think it would be better if Admiral Wedgcroft were left to speak for himself.

ADMIRAL

As you please. I wanted Ferrers to understand what the Service point of view is.

FIRST LORD

Certainly. Shall I put it ? The point is, Ferrers, that some extremely sound officers feel—well, not that the thing's wild-cat—but that it is slow in proving itself. Meanwhile, the Prime Minister and I are behind you. But politicians come and go ; the Navy goes on for ever. Would that represent your brother-in-law's opinion, Helston ?

ADMIRAL

Politely put.

FIRST LORD

But we politicians are sometimes firmer in the saddle than others suppose. The Prime Minister doesn't make a habit of resigning. As you grow older, resignation seems less and less productive. You can take it that the Admiralty are backing you, Ferrers.

FERRERS

I'm grateful. But I see Wedgcroft's argument. I'm expensive. Workshops. Foundry. Destroyers for patrol. Two cruisers. A power station. Wireless. A squadron of aeroplanes. As every month passes in Whitehall " extremely sound officers " add up the bill. I don't blame them. The question is : how long will it last ?

FIRST LORD

As long as my confidence in you lasts.

FERRERS

(*After a moment's thought*)

Why do you, sir, believe in me in that way ?

FIRST LORD

Why do your shipmates here believe in you ? It is a power some men possess.

FERRERS

(*Returning eagerly to the point he was making*)

It's not so much me personally, as the idea. It's their belief in the thing itself that holds us together.

FIRST LORD

An act of faith.

FERRERS

What's more—a continuing act. Not the burst of enthusiasm that makes a bank-clerk enlist or a woman run off to a new faith-healer, but day after day, month after month. . . . There's not a man here that hasn't a touch of genius of his own—but they have to work on my lines ; cancel their work at my order ; sweat for days, and then, because I want to try out another possibility, break up all they've done and start again.

ADMIRAL

Isn't that plain obedience to orders ?

FERRERS

No, sir. It's less simple. It's subjecting your imagination to orders. Nothing on God's earth is harder to men of imagination. There's only one thing makes it possible—an absolute acceptance and, within the stress of the job itself, singleness of mind. That's what the girl would destroy.

FIRST LORD

Necessarily ? Because she's a woman ?

ADMIRAL

You mean, there would be jealousies, Ferrers ?

FERRERS

No, sir. There might be. That's not the point.

FIRST LORD

Not?

FERRERS

I wish I could make you see, sir. We carry on by one saving grace—by knowing and feeling the difference between on duty and off duty. A woman can't. She can obey or she can think for herself. She can be a subordinate or an independent human being. Magnificent as each. But she can't, for months at a stretch, be *both* in relation to the same man. My officers can be and are. A woman doesn't divide up her mind as we divide ours. If I suggested to Carr that he should do something he didn't believe in, he would argue and criticize. So he should. That's what he's here for. If I gave him an order, he'd obey. That obedience would be final and absolute—nothing personal about it. The girl might obey too. I dare say she would. But it would give her a sense of—not rebellion but of—inferiority. Either she'd begin to enjoy it and become a slave, like a whipped dog, or she'd nurse her personal criticism to poison her Service obedience. A woman is a personal animal. That's her greatness. At her best, she cuts through shams and clichés—she's a personal realist— as we can't be. But this particular job needs——

FIRST LORD

Go on, Ferrers. What does it need?

FERRERS

(This carries the whole emphasis of the play and is spoken very slowly, clearly, quietly)

I think the rarest thing in the world, sir—impersonal passion.

FIRST LORD

Thank you. I am glad I interrupted my journey to Buenos Aires. You have answered your own question : why do I believe in you ? *(After a pause)* But—" impersonal passion " ? There are women who have been great saints.

ADMIRAL

Bless my soul, this girl isn't——

FIRST LORD

No, Admiral, as you shrewdly observe, probably she is not. But the great female saints have not all been, as women, cold. . . . Really, you naval officers take an extremely odd view of the sex. You recognize no intervening territory between Belgrave Square and the shady side of Burlington Street. You put all your money on matrimony or the mantelpiece.

ADMIRAL

It seems to work.

FIRST LORD

With ladies themselves ? Of course it does. You act upon the principle that some women live by falling on their feet ; the rest by—assuming a different posture ; naturally they like to know which attitude is expected of them. It prevents confusion and shortens procedure. But though such maritime distinctions do, no doubt, facilitate the Navy's silent progress from drawing-room to alcove, they are the ruin of philosophy. You mustn't assume, Admiral, that because a girl has bright eyes the angels have lost interest in her.

ADMIRAL

Angels my foot ! Why are we talking of angels ? (KAREN *and* BRISSING *return to the verandah. They do not enter the room and those on the stage do not see them.*)

FIRST LORD

Because they are extremely relevant. Do you suggest, Ferrers, that women haven't the capacity for impersonal passion ? No religieuses ? No artists ? No women of science ? . . . . No mathematicians ? . . . Come.

FERRERS

They may be capable of it in relation to a God they worship.

FIRST LORD

And to a picture they paint ? And to a poem they write ? . . .

FERRERS

This isn't her picture. It's mine. And I'm not God. (KAREN *enters with* BRISSING *behind her but hesitates. A sudden silence. Seeing that she is eavesdropping, she turns to go out. Enter* DENHAM.)

DENHAM

(*To* FERRERS)

Master-at-Arms reports fort cleared up for rounds, sir.

FERRERS

Take rounds for me, Brissing.

BRISSING

(*To* DENHAM)

Waiting now?

DENHAM

Yes, sir.

BRISSING

(*To* KAREN)

Sorry, I must go the rounds. (BRISSING *follows* DENHAM *out by door* R. KAREN *returns to verandah.*

FIRST LORD

Women who vanish when they're not wanted are rare. . . . Well, Ferrers?

FERRERS

If I do what you ask, sir, there's no going back.

FIRST LORD

If you don't, there's no going forward. See her, Ferrers.

ADMIRAL

(*Looking round and seeing* KAREN *on verandah*)

I'll bring her in. (*He goes out.*)

FIRST LORD

See her.   That's all I ask.

FERRERS

I have seen her.

FIRST LORD

What?

FERRERS

I said : I *have* seen her.

FIRST LORD
(*Serious*)

Ah ! . . . (*Then on the principle that the only way to treat a serious emotion is lightly*) Historians tell us, my dear Ferrers, that, on appropriate occasions, ladies and gentlemen of the Middle Ages shared the same bed but placed a sword between them.

FERRERS

Did no one ever put the sword into its sheath ? Human nature must have changed. (FIRST LORD *has moved up stage, meets* ADMIRAL *as he enters with* KAREN. *Sound of chatter from bridge-players.* SANDFORD *comes in, takes two drinks off the table.*)

ADMIRAL

Who's winning, Sandford ?

SANDFORD

We are, sir.

99

ADMIRAL

You and——

SANDFORD

Lady Helston, sir.

ADMIRAL

Thank God for that. (*Exit* SANDFORD).

FIRST LORD
(*To* KAREN)

Is there a good view from the signal station ?

KAREN

You can hear the water sucking into the coves under the cliff. It makes you want to throw yourself in.

FIRST LORD

Come, Helston. If I were drowned, that would be most unfortunate. You shall go with me and prevent a bye-election in the East Riding. My majority is only seventy-two. (ADMIRAL *and* FIRST LORD *go out.* FERRERS *has seated himself at the big table.* KAREN *comes forward, but he does not look at her and she is left stranded in mid-stage. She would go out, but suddenly he says :*)

FERRERS

Come here, please. (*She obeys and stands beside him, but at a little distance, waiting. Then he looks at her—a long gaze—and jerks his head away. From now onward he is forcing himself to speak to her strictly on Service, as he would to a junior officer—and he leaves her standing.*)

FERRERS

You work in the Green Hill Observatory ?

KAREN

Yes.

FERRERS

For how long ?

KAREN

Three years now.

FERRERS

You like it ?

KAREN

I love it.   It's the nearest thing to pure mathematics anyone has ever been paid for.

FERRERS

Who's your chief ?

KAREN

Sir Henry Savernake.

FERRERS

How old is he ?

KAREN

Seventy-four.

FERRERS

And you ?

KAREN

Thirty.

FERRERS

Not twenty-nine ?

KAREN

Thirty. (*A smile*) I always tell the truth about mathematics.

FERRERS

So I see. (*Pause.*)

KAREN

Are there more questions ?

FERRERS

I'm afraid so.

KAREN

May I sit down ?

FERRERS

Of course. I'm sorry. (*He rises, but she seats herself at once on the arm of a chair. He sits again.*)

KAREN
(*A smile*)

You can assume that I am standing—for drill purposes.

FERRERS

What do you know of " drill purposes " ?

KAREN

It's a phrase Mr. Brissing has just taught me.   (*Pause.*)

FERRERS

Miss Selby, it has been suggested that you should take your brother's place.

KAREN

(*It is not a question*)

Here.

FERRERS

For many reasons I'm against it ; I dare say you are. But we're in a hole.   There's no one else to do the job, and the job must be done.   The First Lord pressed me. I promised to talk it over with you.   You would receive your brother's pay and allowances.   You know what they were ?

KAREN

Yes.

FERRERS

Enough ?

KAREN

More than I get.

FERRERS

I take it you'd lodge with Lady Helston.

KAREN

Does she know ?

FERRERS

Not yet.

KAREN

What will she say when she does ?

FERRERS

Does that matter ?

KAREN

Not to me. . . . All right.   Go on.

FERRERS

You would lodge with her but live in this mess, as a member of it, and work under my orders.

KAREN

I understand.

FERRERS

If the thing's impossible, say so.   We'll leave it at that.

KAREN

It is not impossible. . . . What will my work be ?

FERRERS

(*Surprised*)

What *would* it be ?

KAREN

That door leads to the Control Room ?   My brother worked in there.   (*She looks round the room.*)

FERRERS

He and I worked together. . . . What are you looking at?

KAREN

It's all new to-night.   Soon I shall know every scar on
the leather of this chair.   And the ink-stain on that desk.
Whose desk is it?

FERRERS

Brissing's.

KAREN

(*Looking towards the other desk*)
And Mr. Sandford there?   (*And towards the Control
Room.*)   Is that a special lock?

FERRERS

The door of the Control Room needs two keys,
used together.   I carried one; your brother the second;
Carr has it now. . . . There's no reason you shouldn't
smoke.   Will you?

KAREN

I'd rather not—yet.

FERRERS

Is there—anything else you'd like?   I forget this is
a party.

KAREN

Nothing.   I want you to forget.

FERRERS

(*Relieved*)

Thank you.   Then we can get on.   You know what kind of work we do here ?

KAREN

Roughly.   Anti-aircraft.

FERRERS

You have heard people speak of Scorpions ?

KAREN

Since I came here.

FERRERS

Your brother didn't write of them ?

KAREN

Never.

FERRERS

Good ; but he might have without real harm.   The word's a nickname—a cover—no more.   Scorpions are a form of aerial torpedo.   The object is to destroy enemy aircraft—but not by direct hits.   You grasp that ?

KAREN

Not yet.

FERRERS

To hit an aeroplane with a shell is the devil.   His speed's too great ; he turns too fast.   Scorpions work on a different principle.   They're not shells fired from a gun to hit or miss.   They move under their own power, as a torpedo does in the water. Roughly speaking, what they are is very small high-speed aeroplanes without a pilot. They carry a high explosive charge. *And they follow the enemy in the air——*

KAREN

How—follow?

FERRERS

First, by wireless steering from the ground, you get the torpedo within reach of the enemy. Then the whole point of the thing is this. The torpedo is fitted with sensitive receivers—two sets of them. The vibration of the enemy affects one set and moves the torpedo's rudders. The enemy may twist and turn like a hare, but a Scorpion has the legs of the fastest machine designed and moves continually towards the centre of vibration—follows it in the air. When near enough, it explodes.

KAREN

As though the enemy were a magnet, drawing the torpedo on to itself?

FERRERS

In effect, yes.

KAREN

I see. What makes the Scorpion explode when you want it to?

FERRERS

Again, the enemy vibrations acting on the second set of receivers. They detonate the charge.

KAREN

If the enemy cuts out his engine, what then?

FERRERS

He loses speed. He can't manœuvre. If he does it often, the fighters get him.

KAREN

What about interference from other machines in the air and your own vibrations?

FERRERS

Four seconds!

KAREN

What—four seconds?

FERRERS

To see that snag. You're quick. Do you see the way out—how to eliminate?

KAREN

Not yet.

FERRERS

It took us three months.

KAREN

It's done, then.

FERRERS

Your brother found that. Yes, it's done.

KAREN

Even then, doesn't the effect of vibration vary with the type of engine?

FERRERS

How much do you know of the mathematics of vibration? (*Enter* LADY HELSTON.)

LADY HELSTON
(*Echoing*)

How much *do* you know, Miss Selby, of the mathematics of vibration? Really, Edward, are you bullying her already?

FERRERS
(*Rising reluctantly*)

Your bridge isn't over yet?

LADY HELSTON

Dickie's gone to fetch a wrap I left in the car. (*Sits down.*) Give me a cigarette. (*To* KAREN) It sounded as if you were being given a lesson. But I'd forgotten— you are quite a mathematician yourself! I was rather good at it at school, but of course one can't keep up everything. Edward said once that mathematics were a form of poetry. (*To* FERRERS) Didn't you?

FERRERS

I was very foolish if I said that to you. But you can't have invented it. (*He lights her cigarette.*)

LADY HELSTON

Thank you. You do know how to light a cigarette,

Edward. I give you marks for that. Did you learn that in your monastery ?

FERRERS

I learnt it from a woman, who, if you give her a chance, always pokes her nose into a flame.

LADY HELSTON
(*To* KAREN)

You see ? I told you he was like that. I don't know what it means, but didn't it sound fierce ? I expect that was because I interrupted the lesson. Couldn't it go on ?

KAREN

I'm afraid you'd find it dull.

LADY HELSTON

Not as dull as you think. I know him better than you do. He has all the virtues—except that he won't learn.

FERRERS

What ought I to learn ?

LADY HELSTON
(*Counting on her fingers*)

Well, first, which side your bread is buttered. Brian said in his last letter—but, perhaps that's a naval secret.

FERRERS

Then don't pass it on. Sir Brian Wedgcroft is Lady Helston's half-brother, Miss Selby. He happens also to

be Second Sea Lord.   Admirals to right of us.   Admirals
to left of us.   Ours but to do and die.

LADY HELSTON

No need to die, Edward.

FERRERS

Only to do what you tell me.

LADY HELSTON
(*Unperturbed*)

I should adore that.   Like having a tame tiger.   Or
would you eat me ?   I should adore that too.   (*Yawns.*)
I've always thought the lady of Riga had it both ways.

FERRERS
(*Laughing*)

Granted a Freudian tiger.

LADY HELSTON

It must have been.   Everything is.   Specially limer-
icks and nursery rhymes.   Are mathematics Freudian,
Miss Selby ?   Until this evening, I thought they were
completely sexless.

KAREN

But I thought you said you were good at them at
school.

LADY HELSTON

I expect those were what Edward calls pure mathematics.

FERRERS

Didn't they produce results ? Poor Sybil, you must have had a tedious girlhood. Not an admiral in the whole dormitory. Or were you captain of the hockey eleven and the glory of the Guides ?

LADY HELSTON

In fact I was. Edward is always right except when he thinks he is. Tell Miss Selby about her girlhood, Edward. It would interest her enormously. And then you shall take us round.

FERRERS

Round what ?

LADY HELSTON

All the mysteries. (*To* KAREN) You know, on board a warship, they take you everywhere. Conning-tower, turrets, plotting-house, engine-rooms — everywhere. That's the difference between a ship and a house. Civilians take pretty women higher and higher ; naval officers take them lower and lower. Dull women are left on the upper deck ; moderately attractive ones are shown the boiler rooms ; I expect you would be mathematical for hours in the double-bottoms or the bilge. But Edward won't show anyone anything. The workshops yes— lathes and oil and soapy water and the foundry and the Power House and this place, but there's a little holy of holies in there—(*moves towards Control Room*)—that no one has ever gone into until to-night.

FERRERS

Why do you want to ?

LADY HELSTON

Bluebeard.

FERRERS

No, but why *do* you want to ?   It interests me to know.

LADY HELSTON

Shall I tell you ?   Because you're so stubborn about it.   It's such a silly mystery.   Can you tell me why you don't want me to ?

FERRERS

I can, but it wouldn't seem a reason to you.

LADY HELSTON

Do you think I'm going to steal a secret formula ?

FERRERS

You wouldn't know which to steal.

LADY HELSTON

Well ?

FERRERS

It's where I work.   It's where I think and imagine. It's where everything else is shut out.

LADY HELSTON

But Carr and Brissing and Dickie—they come in.

113

FERRERS

Sometimes—on duty. Nothing personal comes there. I don't want to refuse things to you—but don't ask this. There is such a thing as an absolute rule. Think I'm a fool if you like, but try to see what kind of a fool I am.

LADY HELSTON

I don't think you a fool, but I think you are stubborn and proud. I've never heard of such a thing! The Admiral's wife asks—*asks*—to be shown into your Control Room and you blankly refuse. Well, my dear Edward, this time you can't refuse.

KAREN

I'm sorry. It's nothing to do with me. But I do see what he means, Lady Helston. It does mean a lot sometimes, when you are doing a particular kind of work, to have a room——

LADY HELSTON

It's very kind of you to agree with him. But as it happens, just for once, he's going to agree with me.

FERRERS

I'm sorry. I'm really sorry. But I'm not. Don't press it.

LADY HELSTON

It happens to be the Admiral's order.

FERRERS

Do you mean that?

LADY HELSTON

I asked him before dinner. He said I could go in. Now what do you say?

FERRERS

That was not an effective order. It isn't one he could possibly give.

LADY HELSTON

And why not?

FERRERS

Sybil, don't go on with this. Let's forget it.

LADY HELSTON

Answer my question. Why isn't it an order he could possibly give?

FERRERS

Because he can't give as a reason for my resignation that he ordered me to admit his wife into my Control Room. If you were in your senses——

LADY HELSTON

Do you mean you'd resign rather than let me in?

FERRERS

It would never come to that. I have told you—the order is one he couldn't possibly give. Now, please, forget it.

LADY HELSTON

(*Very quietly*)

I have a good memory. You had better go on with

your mathematics while you have time. (SANDFORD
appears in verandah with her cloak.)

SANDFORD

Here it is.   Will you put it on now?

LADY HELSTON

I will.   (*She sweeps out.*)

KAREN

Can't you do anything?   That is really dangerous.

FERRERS

As much to you as to me.

KAREN

I wondered whether you knew that.   (FERRERS *takes
a drink.*)

FERRERS

How much do you know of the mathematics of
vibration?

KAREN

As it happens, a lot.

FERRERS

But not as a specialist?

KAREN

As a specialist.

FERRERS

How?   How did you come to it?

KAREN

By way of music.   I spent a year once on the vibration of strings.

FERRERS

My God, is that true ?

KAREN

Does it seem foolish ?

FERRERS

(*He comes over to her*)

Go on.   Go on.   I want to hear this.

KAREN

Mathematics is a cold thing to most people.   It's not to me. . . . (*She breaks off.*)   Probably, if I go on, you will—not want to use me. . . . You see——

FERRERS

Get on.   Get on.

KAREN

People think it mad—anyhow in a woman—to be a mathematician.   Even mathematicians themselves think that—some of them.   They look at me.   I know what they're thinking.   " You ! "—because I'm not ugly—and not cold.   As if they'd found me selling matches or scrubbing floors.   And others think I'm not doing my job in the world.   They want me to use my brains their way—converting someone, compelling someone—politics, economics, anti-war.   For me to shut myself up in the Green Hill Observatory seems to

117

them just funk—an escape from life. If you won't march in one of their regiments you are always accused of escaping from life. Mathematics isn't that to me. It's one of the ways of listening. It's one of the ways of being and loving. One of the ways. They don't want to listen. They want to shout and compel. But the world is growing tired of the regiments. They fail everywhere. The misery they want to cure by force is the misery they have created by force—and will create again. Suddenly men and women will grow tired of marching in step and shouting choruses. We shall listen when we are still. The world is beginning to listen again. It is beginning to watch again. In poetry, the thing comes through words. Music says it direct. Saints and lovers know it. And mathematics . . . I want to listen; I must communicate but not through words. And mathematics, to me—oh, the agony of trying to say in words what can only be said— (*she is laughing and almost crying*). But I needn't say it to you. You *know*—don't you?

FERRERS

You must never say it to me—if we are to work here together.

KAREN

I never shall again. But you had to know whether I am—the kind of—mathematician you can work with.

FERRERS

The only kind. (*Long pause.*) Do you understand what it would mean—your living here?

KAREN

I think so.

FERRERS

An absolute discipline—you, me, all of us.

KAREN

I accept that.   Why are you afraid ?

FERRERS

You are a woman men desire.   That's the danger.

KAREN

I desire men.   Isn't that the safety ?

FERRERS

Safety ?   You could drive them mad.

KAREN

Cold women drive them mad.   It's they who dangle and bait and hang out for a price.   They can despise men's desire because they don't share it.   It's their vanity ; they can't cut it out.   They tease an agony to keep themselves alive.   Hasn't the Navy a word for them ?

FERRERS

It has.

KAREN

Now are you beginning to know me ?

FERRERS

Tell me one thing more.   When we met—before

dinner—you said your brother had never sent home photographs.   Why did you say that?

KAREN

It just—came out.

FERRERS

You saw a physical likeness between me and—what you had expected?

KAREN

Not so much physical. . . . I don't know. . . . Yes, even that I suppose.   It was queer—wasn't it?

FERRERS

Our meeting?

KAREN

Our recognizing each other.

FERRERS

I knew without looking at you.   I knew the feel of the air about you.

KAREN

I knew before I came in.   (CARR, FLAG CAPTAIN, LADY HELSTON, ADMIRAL, FIRST LORD *and* SANDFORD *have come in from verandah.   The party is about to break up. General buzz of conversation.*)

ADMIRAL

Well, my dear, ready to start?   (SANDFORD *gets* LADY HELSTON'S *cloak and holds it out.*)   You had a pretty good evening.   What did you win?

LADY HELSTON

I left it on the table. I thought you would pick it up.

ADMIRAL

(*Opening his fist*)

And so I did. Here you are. (*Counts money into* LADY HELSTON's *palm*.) Fourteen and sixpence.

LADY HELSTON

What do you expect me to do with that ? (CARR *goes out to verandah*.)

ADMIRAL

Well——

LADY HELSTON

I haven't my bag.

ADMIRAL

Your bag——

LADY HELSTON

On the table. Didn't you see it ?

FERRERS

(*An irritable order*)

Bag. (*But* CARR, *ever watchful, has brought it and hands it to her*.)

CARR

Is this it ?

LADY HELSTON

Thank you. Could someone give me a note for all this silver ? (*They begin to search for a note in their pockets.* SANDFORD *is still holding out the cloak. It is* CARR *who finds a note.*)

CARR

I have a note, I think. (LADY HELSTON *begins to count out money on the table.*)

FERRERS

Sandford.

SANDFORD

What ?

FERRERS

Down masts and sails. (SANDFORD *throws cloak over his arm and sits.*)

ADMIRAL

Now. We really must be getting on. Ferrers, your decision in the morning ?

FERRERS

I have made it, sir.

ADMIRAL

Yes, yes, but it will keep. (*To* FIRST LORD) I hope we haven't tired you, sir. It's getting late.

FIRST LORD

Not at all. I think it has been a most successful evening. I hope you agree, Ferrers ?

FERRERS

It's stopping too soon. (FIRST LORD *moves down to* FERRERS *and* KAREN.)

ADMIRAL

(*To* BRISSING)

The car's there ?

BRISSING

Yes, sir.

FLAG CAPTAIN

I'll go on ahead.   I want to look at my tail lamp.
Good night, Ferrers.

FERRERS

Good night, sir.

FLAG CAPTAIN

You'll be my passenger again, Miss Selby ?

KAREN

Please.   I'll follow you out.   (*Exit* FLAG CAPTAIN, R.
BRISSING *goes with him.*)

FERRERS

(*To* KAREN)

Must you ?

KAREN

What ?

FERRERS

Go.   I want to show you the Control Room.   Carr,
have you the key—— (*The* FIRST LORD *checks him.*
CARR *seems not to hear.*)

CARR
(*To* LADY HELSTON)

I'm very sorry.   No one seems to have a ten-shilling note.   (*Reluctantly*) There's a pound.

LADY HELSTON

That will do.   Thank you.   (*Gives him the silver.*) Now I owe you—what?   Four and six?   Is that right, Miss Selby?

KAREN

Five and six.

LADY HELSTON

Oh, thank you.   I'm not a mathematician.

ADMIRAL

Now are we all set?

LADY HELSTON

If I might have my cloak.   (FIRST LORD *takes it from* SANDFORD.)

FIRST LORD
(*Politely impatient*)

Let me.   (*She puts it on.*)

FERRERS
(*To* KAREN)

Well, to-morrow.   Can you start work then?

KAREN

I will.

124

FERRERS

She won't head you off?

KAREN

No.

FERRERS

She will if she can.

KAREN

No.   I promise.   Good night.

FERRERS

Good night.

LADY HELSTON

Who will do what if she can?

FIRST LORD
(*Quickly*)

Good night, Ferrers.

FERRERS

Good night, sir.   And thank you.

FIRST LORD

Ah, well.   It's pleasant to be thanked for getting one's own way.

FERRERS

I have mine too—as far as I can see it.

LADY HELSTON
(*To* FERRERS)

Good night.   I think it has been a charming conspiracy. (*To* ADMIRAL) It will give us something to talk about on the way home. (*General good nights from which, as they drift towards the door, the following emerge.*)

SANDFORD
(*To* LADY HELSTON)

I'll see you out.

LADY HELSTON

You overbid that last time, Dickie.

SANDFORD

Did I? I thought my diamonds——

LADY HELSTON

Well, never mind. I don't mind losing.

SANDFORD

But you won. . . . You've left your bag. (*Retrieves it.*)

CARR
(*To* KAREN)

I owe you a shilling.

KAREN

Me? . . . Oh, I see.

CARR

I'd have let her get away with it.

KAREN

I was afraid you would.

CARR

And may I say I'm glad—about the other thing?

KAREN

I hoped you might feel that. . . . I didn't even hope you'd say it.   Until to-morrow then.

CARR

To-morrow.

LADY HELSTON
(*From door*)

Are you coming with us?

KAREN

Which would be easier for you?   Captain Winter asked me——

LADY HELSTON

Very well.   (LADY HELSTON, ADMIRAL *and* SANDFORD *go out.*)

FIRST LORD
(*To* KAREN)

I wish I were coming with you.

KAREN

You mean there'll be questions.

FIRST LORD

Well, she has to be told some time.   Good night, Carr . . . Ferrers. (FIRST LORD *and* KAREN *go out.* CARR *goes at once to the drawer in which he put away his*

127

letter.   Takes it out, sits at table, unscrews his fountain pen, begins to write.   Meanwhile—)

FERRERS

Now the damned party's over, I wish it wasn't. (*Pause.   * CARR *writes*) I'll get things ready for the morning.   Give me your key.   (CARR *hands him the key and goes on writing.   Sound of cars starting.   * FERRERS *jangles two keys in his hand.   Restless, irresolute.   Goes to Selby's water colour and peers at it.*)   She doesn't paint, does she ?   (*Enter* BRISSING *on the silence.*)

BRISSING

She doesn't need to. (*Silence.   He mixes two whiskies and sodas from a hissing siphon.   Outside the sentry sounds six bells.*)   That girl has a flank like a race-horse. (FERRERS *turns.   * BRISSING *holds out a whiskey and soda to him, offering it.   * FERRERS *shakes his head and points to* CARR.   BRISSING *puts the drink at* CARR'S *elbow.   * CARR *looks up, nods, returns to writing.*) 'Night.   I'll turn in.   (BRISSING *goes out* R. *carrying his whiskey.*)

FERRERS

Still writing home ? . . . Keep dogs there ?

CARR

Pair of retrievers.   (FERRERS *sits down on arm of chair.   * CARR *takes a gulp of drink, and continues to write as the Curtain falls.*)

ACT II

ACT II

Scene 1

The Same. Nearly four months later; early July. Just before eleven in the morning. Hotter weather. Loose covers of Service pattern—white with blue piping at edges. SANDFORD *and* BRISSING, *at their desks, working at plans. Since the party, the furniture has been moved. The settee is* L. *The long table is down stage* R. *Plans lie on it to which both* SANDFORD *and* BRISSING *from time to time refer. The dress of the day is full whites, but the officers, while working, wear, within limits, what they please. Silence when the Curtain rises.*

SANDFORD
(Tired, driving himself, on edge)
The thing won't fit. If he wants the fulcrum of spindle 84 at point six-two of its length, any conceivable gadget will foul the compensating mechanism.

BRISSING
(Without turning from his own work)
You'd better conceive a gadget that won't.

SANDFORD
(Goes over to BRISSING, *paper in hand)*
But look at this——

BRISSING

For God's sake, go to hell.

(SANDFORD *returns to his desk. Silence. After a time* BRISSING *lays down his own pen.*)

BRISSING

Now what's the trouble ?

SANDFORD

This (*at table*). Fulcrum at point six-two. As far as I can see the spindle action depends on that. If we shift it a hair's breadth, the whole of his new calculation series loses its effect.

BRISSING

It's not Ferrers' ; it's hers.

SANDFORD

She works damned fine—like painting a miniature. It may not be necessary to carry precision so far. We can ask her.

BRISSING

She's not back. Ferrers kept her at it all night or nearly. She didn't push off until five this morning.

SANDFORD

The man's mad.

BRISSING

He works himself harder.

SANDFORD

That isn't the point.   Karen turns up at the Helston's house at all hours.   Sybil hates it.

BRISSING

Does she enter the times in a register ?

SANDFORD

She's often awake.

BRISSING

She would be—and she would tell you.

SANDFORD

It's not because———

BRISSING

Dry up.   I'm not going to quarrel with you about Lady H.   Let's get back to this spindle of yours.

SANDFORD

No.   You say things and then run away from them. What have you against her ?   In a way, as Karen's hostess, she is responsible.

BRISSING

(*Mocking*)

In a way, as Karen's hostess, she *is* responsible.

SANDFORD

If there's a scandal in this place———

133

BRISSING

Who's going to make scandal if she doesn't? Ferrers carries his damned austerity too far. So does Karen. They never touch, even when they're working side by side at the same table. He puts down a T-square; she picks it up from the desk; it's not even handed between them.

SANDFORD

They daren't touch. If they did——

BRISSING

What if they did?

SANDFORD

You'd go mad for one.

BRISSING

I?

SANDFORD

You want her.

BRISSING

I'm not a monk, if that's what you mean.

SANDFORD

You want *her*. I'm not blind. Oh, the love of your life may be in London. Meanwhile Karen——

BRISSING

She's Ferrers'.

134

SANDFORD

If she were—if you knew it—here, now—if you watched it going on—could you work in this place? (*No answer.*)

BRISSING
(*At last*)

Anyhow, Karen does her job.

SANDFORD

Oh, she does her job.

BRISSING

Do you know any other woman who would do it as she does—and not play men up?

SANDFORD

You have it your own way.

BRISSING

Isn't it true?

SANDFORD

No, it's not.   She may think it is.   But she's in love. If Ferrers lifted a finger, she'd go to him to-night.   Sybil says——

BRISSING

My God, can't you keep off that woman?   If she could, she'd break this place because Ferrers won't let her run it.   She may yet.   She has the Admiral in her pocket.   She treats you like a dog and all you do is lick her boots. Ever since Karen has been here—four months now—that woman has used you. You come back here yapping her opinions as if they were your own. You've forgotten they're not your own. "If there's a scandal in this place, she's responsible." Aren't those her words? And who said Karen was willing to be Ferrers' mistress? Lady H. again. She's a candidate herself and you know it.

SANDFORD

(*Trembling with anger*)

Now you can take all that back.

BRISSING

Not a word. . . . She has no use for you except as a poodle on a string.

SANDFORD

Take it back.

BRISSING

I've been wanting to say it for weeks.

SANDFORD

Take it back !

BRISSING

Are you going to fling yourself at me in defence of your lady-love ?

(SANDFORD *springs at* BRISSING *who thrusts him away. He shakes, swerves and collapses.* BRISSING *runs to him and helps him to recover.*)

SANDFORD
(*From table*)

I could have killed you then. Do you know, while I was standing there, I couldn't see your face.

BRISSING

One of the rewards of attempted murder.

SANDFORD

Now, what are you going to do ?

BRISSING

Withdraw, apologize, get on with the job. Come on, Dick. It's the only sanity in this place. (SANDFORD *tries to rise but can't move.*)

SANDFORD

I'm weak as a kitten. . . . I believe I was mad then.

BRISSING

Have a drink. (*He goes to mix it.* FERRERS *comes in.*)

FERRERS

Why drink now ?

137

BRISSING

Dick threw a faint.

FERRERS

Nonsense. (*To* SANDFORD) Stand up. (SANDFORD *stands and sways.* FERRERS *grasps him by both arms.*)

FERRERS

To hell. What *is* this? You look as if you'd been drugged.

SANDFORD

I'm all right, sir. I can go on.

FERRERS

I dare say. . . . Have you two been scrapping?

BRISSING

Let it go, sir.

FERRERS

Why?

BRISSING

Because it went very far and——

FERRERS

How far?

BRISSING

(*Quickly and steadily*)

It went very far and came back again. Please let it go? (*Pause. Six bells are struck.*)

138

FERRERS

Yes. All right. . . . Why aren't you both in the workshops ? I thought you had a bench test this morning.

BRISSING

We have.

FERRERS

At what time ?

BRISSING

Eleven.

FERRERS

It's struck. (*Enter* KAREN.)

FERRERS

Why are you back ? I told you not to come till the afternoon. You haven't had five hours sleep.

KAREN

I thought you wanted me. (*To* SANDFORD) Have you been working on that spindle ?

SANDFORD

I began on it.

KAREN

There's a point I want to show you. I remembered it after I'd gone last night. (*She goes to his desk.*) Look.

FERRERS

Not now. They are due in the workshops. (*To* BRISSING *and* SANDFORD) Better go on. . . . Dick !

SANDFORD

Yes ?

FERRERS

Are you all right ?

SANDFORD

I am now, sir.

FERRERS

Cancel the bench test if necessary. Turn in and sleep.

SANDFORD

I can carry on.

FERRERS

No one's worth swinging for, you know. (*He turns away abruptly and* BRISSING *and* SANDFORD *go out.*)

KAREN

What's wrong ?

FERRERS

Nothing.

KAREN

Shall we work in the Control Room or here ?

FERRERS

Here.   The papers are in my cabin.

KAREN

Have you been up all night ?

FERRERS

I worked upstairs a bit after we'd locked the Control Room.

KAREN

Why not sleep now ?

FERRERS

I'll take it sudden, when I need it.   Get the work. Ring the bell as you go.   (*She goes out to his bedroom, ringing the bell.   Enter* DENHAM.)

FERRERS

I want some water.

DENHAM

Aye, aye, sir.

FERRERS

I thought you were a marine.

DENHAM

I am a marine, sir.

141

FERRERS

Then don't say: "Aye, aye, sir." Everything's "very good" to you.

DENHAM

Very good, sir.

FERRERS

Lucky to be a marine. Have you a kettle boiling ?

DENHAM

Yes, sir.

FERRERS

Bring some tea for Miss Selby. (*Exit* DENHAM. KAREN *returns. Spreads out papers.*)

KAREN

Was that my fault ?

FERRERS

What ?

KAREN

Those two. Something had happened. Had they been quarrelling ?

FERRERS

Not about you. At least—why should they quarrel about you ?

142

KAREN

I wanted to make no difference to this place—except my work.

FERRERS

Then, for God's sake, let's assume you have made none. (*He rises suddenly and takes his cap.*)

KAREN

Where are you going?

FERRERS

Carr's in the Power House. I promised to go over. (BRISSING *comes in.*)

KAREN
(*To* FERRERS)
I thought we were to work together.

FERRERS

I'll go to Carr first.

KAREN

You can't go now.

FERRERS

Indeed I can.

KAREN

I have something to tell you.

FERRERS

It can wait.

143

KAREN

No. It's urgent. Last night——

FERRERS

Get on with your work and leave me to mine !

KAREN

Very well. (*She sits down, her back to him. He moves towards her, almost touches her, turns abruptly away, sees* BRISSING.)

FERRERS

(*To* BRISSING)

What about your bench test ?

BRISSING

Dick's adjustments aren't ready. They'll be a quarter of an hour. (FERRERS *goes out.*)

BRISSING

Why do you stand for it ?

KAREN

Because——

BRISSING

Service ?

KAREN

Yes.

BRISSING

Liar.

KAREN

I said I'd go through with this.

BRISSING

That's no reason he should refuse to listen when you have something to tell him.

KAREN

He and I understand each other.

BRISSING

Or is it that a woman will stand anything from a man she loves ? They say so in books.

KAREN

Do they ? It's not true.

BRISSING

(Quick on his cue)

No, but it is true she'll stand anything if he loves her. Isn't it ? Isn't it ?

KAREN

Ferrers can run this place in his own way.

BRISSING

Not *if* he loves you.

KAREN

What ?

BRISSING

I said : Not if he loves you—as you think he does. Does he ?

145

KAREN

Love me ?

BRISSING

That's what I'm asking. That's what you're beginning to ask yourself. Isn't it ? I've asked it too. I know what it feels like.

KAREN

You ?

BRISSING

About my own girl. She's not faithful to me, you know.

KAREN

How much does that matter ? Did you expect her to be ?

BRISSING

I hoped like a fool.

KAREN

Nearly two years ?

BRISSING

It's two years for me—too.

KAREN

Faithful ?

BRISSING

Women are different.

KAREN

Not all.

BRISSING

I know.   Sorry.   It's hell for you . . . Karen, why
should it be hell for either of us—if you feel as men feel.
Why should it ?   I know I'm not the man you want.
You're not the girl I want—not *the* girl I want.   Still,
when sane people are hungry they have dinner together.
(*She looks at him but doesn't answer.*)   All right.   I've
said it.   Now you can tell me off.

KAREN

You are an odd human being.   Why did you say all
that to me ?

BRISSING

One of us had to.

KAREN

You don't love me.

BRISSING

Did I say I did ?

KAREN
(*Holds out her hand*)
No. . . . Kiss me.

BRISSING

Stand up to be kissed.   (*She obeys.   They kiss.   She
sits down again at the table—rigid.*)

BRISSING

Well ?

KAREN

Five minutes ago that was impossible. It still is.
. . . Just abject starvation. Both of us. (*She drops her
head on the table and begins to sob.*) No, my God, why
should I cry ?

BRISSING

Kiss me again. (*Takes her.*)

KAREN

(*A bleak surrender*)

As much as you like. . . .

BRISSING

And you ?

KAREN

Very well. As much as *I* like.

BRISSING

How much, Karen ? Enough ?

KAREN

(*Perhaps consenting*)

I suppose so.

BRISSING

To-night ? Don't turn your face away. Look at
me. Answer me. (*She quietly releases herself.*)

KAREN

What *are* we ?

148

BRISSING

(*Striding away and turning to speak*)

Oddly enough, we are the people for whom the estate of matrimony was ordained. " That have not the gift of continency."

KAREN

The *gift* ? Does the Prayer Book say that ?

BRISSING

It does—though the modern priests tried to cut it out. (*Enter* DENHAM *with tea.*)

KAREN

What's this, Denham ? I didn't order tea.

DENHAM

Commander did, Miss. Water for himself. Tea for you.

KAREN

I see. . . . Thank you, Denham ; I need it. (*Exit* DENHAM.)

KAREN

(*Passing her hand across her forehead*)

That's coming up to breathe !

BRISSING

And think ?

KAREN

Yes.

149

BRISSING

Do you want to think ? (*Pause.*)

KAREN

Do something for me.

BRISSING

You have a habit of not answering questions.

KAREN

If there isn't an answer.

BRISSING

Will there be an answer to-night ? . . . Will there, Karen ? (*She moves the tea-tray and does not answer.*)

KAREN

Do something for me.

BRISSING

What is it ?

KAREN

When's your bench test ?

BRISSING
(*Looking at watch*)

Five minutes.

KAREN

Go to the Power House. Find Ferrers. Make him listen. He thought what I had to say about Lady

Helston was something—personal to us.   It's not.   Last night—early this morning, rather—when I got back, she was waiting for me.   She has made the Admiral choose the earlier date—for the trial.

BRISSING

But he——

KAREN

It gives us short of a month.

BRISSING

But Ferrers postponed it.

KAREN

The Admiral won't forward the postponement.   His message to the Admiralty will go to-night.

BRISSING

But it's mad !   Sandford and I can't be ready.

KAREN

You'll have to be unless the Admiral can be made to change his mind.   He's coming here this morning.

BRISSING

He—here !   Why ?

KAREN

Why not ?

BRISSING

Couldn't he send for Ferrers ?

KAREN

Not when he feels guilty. It salves his conscience this way. He likes to be liked. . . . But Ferrers must know.

BRISSING

He must indeed. I'll tell him. (*Exit* BRISSING. KAREN *pours herself out tea and is settling down to her papers when* SANDFORD *comes in.*)

SANDFORD

(*To the absent* BRISSING)
We're all set. (*To* KAREN) Where's Brissing ?

KAREN

The Power House.

SANDFORD

But he ought to be in the workshops. We're held up.

KAREN

You'll have to hold up a bit longer. (*Looking straight at him*) Did you know we were to run the trial in one month ?

SANDFORD

Two.

KAREN

One. Lady Helston told me early this morning. . . . How long have you known ?

SANDFORD

I knew that Sybil wanted——

KAREN

Did you tell her you needed an extra month on your detonator receivers ?

SANDFORD

I told her the whole damned thing.   I don't suppose she listened but I made it as clear as I could for babes and sucklings.   I said : The receivers, because we've got them placed wrong, are subject to screening and interference.

KAREN

Did that amuse her ?   It doesn't sound like an amorous conversation.

SANDFORD

She said : " Well, can't you place them right ? "   She just can't grasp what it means.   But when I told her that my job was to shift things about inside the Scorpion so that the detonating receivers could be repositioned, she saw that.   " Like repacking a trunk," she said.

KAREN

Poor Dick.   Did you tell her you needed more than a month to repack your trunk ?

SANDFORD

Yes, I did.

KAREN

It made no odds ?

SANDFORD

On the contrary.

KAREN

I see. . . . But did you warn Ferrers that time was to be cut down ?

SANDFORD

There was nothing to warn him about.   Nothing was fixed.

KAREN

And you still love her ?

SANDFORD

That seems mad to you ?

KAREN

No.   Men can love women they despise.   There aren't any rules.   (*Enter* FERRERS, CARR, BRISSING.)

SANDFORD
(*To* BRISSING)

You promised to be back ten minutes ago.   They're all standing by.

FERRERS

For what ?

SANDFORD

The bench test.

FERRERS

Wash it out.   I want you here.   (*Goes to bell and rings.*)   Is that my water ?   (*Drinks.*)   Brissing, get the Admiral's house.   Find out where he is.   If he's there, ask if I can come down to see him at once.   (BRISSING *makes telephone call.   Enter* DENHAM.)

FERRERS

Send down to the workshops.   Tell them Mr. Sandford and Mr. Brissing's bench test must wait.

DENHAM

Is that all, sir ?

FERRERS

Yes.

DENHAM

Very good, sir.   (*Exit* DENHAM.)

FERRERS

Now.   Sit down, please.

BRISSING
(*On telephone*)

Do you know where he is ? . . . All right, thank you.
(*To* FERRERS) He's on his way here, sir.

FERRERS

Very well.   We must think quickly.   You all know
what the position is.   (*To* KAREN) Does Sandford know ?

KAREN

I have just told him.

FERRERS

I want your opinions.   Carr ?

155   L

CARR

(*Slowly and deliberately*)

For the full trial we need six completed Scorpions—more if possible. The bodies are complete, the engines are fitted ; what remains——

FERRERS

No, Carr, I'm sorry. Usually I bless your leisurely methods ; they keep us sane. But there's no time. The point is : I have asked for a postponement to September 12. The Admiral is tying me to the date we originally fixed, four weeks from now, August 9. Can it be done—or not ?

CARR

If you mean, can my wireless be ready—the answer is : yes.

FERRERS

Good. . . . Brissing ?

BRISSING

Well, sir, from this point onwards, Sandford and I more or less work together. I think we can get the vibrational steering to work on the reduced power. That's O.K. if you come in on it.

FERRERS

I ?

BRISSING

And Karen.

FERRERS

I see.   Aren't you giving too much credit to what she and I can do ?   Remember, there's less than four weeks. I don't like the look of it.   Anyhow we've left Sandford's department out of account.

SANDFORD

That's a real snag—the detonator mechanism.   The Lord knows how long that will take.   We're on it now, sir (*bending over his plan*).   That spindle takes up space. It seemed all right before, but if I shift it——

FERRERS

Is it coming ?

SANDFORD

I shall probably have the new drawing out to-morrow or the next day.   Then we have to manufacture.   Then test.   If it's not a go, we have to start again.

FERRERS

In which case, a month won't be enough ?

SANDFORD

No, sir.

FERRERS

Two months ?

SANDFORD

With reasonable luck.   There's nothing wrong in principle.   It's a question of trial and error to get the positions right.

FERRERS

Very well.   Do I accept the earlier date or not?

BRISSING

No, sir!   If you stand up to him, he'll give in.   He's not doing this off his own bat.

FERRERS

Dick?

SANDFORD

I don't know.   You decide, sir.   I'll get it through somehow.   I'll *make* the damned thing work.

CARR

My deliberate view is—I wouldn't be rushed, Ferrers. We've been on this job nearly two years.   It's madness, for the sake of an extra month.

FERRERS

May be.   But this isn't an easy bluff, Carr. If I refuse to run the trial on August 9 and the Admiral sticks his heels in——

SANDFORD

(*Unexpectedly*)

I warn you.   He will.   (*They all look at him.*)   He won't budge.   He's been holding out against this.   He's been holding out like hell.   And now he has given in— he won't go back.   Sybil will see he doesn't.   And the wind at the Admiralty blows her way.

158

FERRERS

There you are, then, Carr. That's the choice. Either I accept August 9 or—we must be prepared to pack up this place.

CARR

(*With steady determination*)

As I see it, it's a matter of principle. Pack and be damned.

BRISSING

I'm with you.

FERRERS

You haven't spoken, Karen.

KAREN

I take your orders, sir.

FERRERS

Then we are decided.

CARR

Are you ?   (*Enter* DENHAM.)

FERRERS

Well ?

DENHAM

The Admiral, sir.   And his lady.

BRISSING

And his lady ?

159

FERRERS

Brissing, go and bring him in.   Don't encourage her.
Perhaps he'll have the grace to leave her in the car.
(*Exeunt* BRISSING *and* DENHAM.)

CARR

But if we know she's there——

FERRERS

For once we can forget it.   Damn it, she can't do us
more harm than she's done.   (*Silence while they wait.*
Enter ADMIRAL *and* BRISSING.   *They all rise.*)

ADMIRAL
(*Nervous and affable*)

Good morning, gentlemen.   Good morning, Miss
Selby.

FERRERS

Good morning, sir.

ADMIRAL

I wanted a word with you, Ferrers.

FERRERS

Alone, sir ?

ADMIRAL

N-no.   Better with all of you, since you're here.

FERRERS

I've been on the telephone to your house, sir.   You

had already left. I was suggesting that I should come to you.

ADMIRAL

To me ? About what ?

FERRERS

The same subject, sir.

ADMIRAL

But this is a matter——

FERRERS

Not new to us, sir.

ADMIRAL

I don't understand you, Ferrers.

FERRERS

Lady Helston gave Miss Selby her orders at five o'clock this morning.

ADMIRAL

Eh ? Oh, that may be. That may be. I believe I did mention it to her. (*Silence.*) Well, gentlemen, I knew this wouldn't come easy to you. That's why I preferred to come up here and have it out with you myself. As you know, for some time past the Admiralty has been pressing me very hard. They feel that these experiments have—— Anyhow, Ferrers, August 9 was originally your own date. Then you ask for postponement to September 12. How do I know you won't ask for a further postponement to October or November ?

FERRERS

That's always possible.

ADMIRAL

You see how difficult— Is there any reason we shouldn't sit down and talk this out man to man? I want you, gentlemen, to accept this as I accept it. We all have to adjust our plans from time to time. I want there to be no sense of injustice. If there's a difference between us——

FERRERS

There's nothing to discuss, sir. As I see it. (*Enter* LADY HELSTON. *They rise, except* KAREN. *Silence, resenting her presence. Even* LADY HELSTON *is a little embarrassed.*)

LADY HELSTON

Good morning, everyone. George—

ADMIRAL

No, no, my dear! You can't come in here.

LADY HELSTON

But, George—it's like an oven in the car——

ADMIRAL

I'm very sorry, my dear, but——

LADY HELSTON

I simply wanted somewhere cool to sit.

ADMIRAL

But not in here, my dear.   We're discussing a Service matter.   Ferrers, is there——— ?

LADY HELSTON

I suppose there is no objection to my sitting on the verandah ?

ADMIRAL
(*Ushering her out*)
No, none whatever, as long as———

LADY HELSTON

I'll go right to the other end—you needn't think———

ADMIRAL

That's not the point. (*She is gone.*) I'm sorry, gentlemen.   You, Ferrers—you were saying———

FERRERS

In my view, sir, there's nothing to discuss.   I understand your decision is that we are to run the trial on August 9.   Very well, that leaves me with one course open.

ADMIRAL

Now, Ferrers, don't be hasty.   Don't say what we shall all regret. I admit you have been— Still, the interests of the Service come first.   There must be no question of resignation. We are naval officers, not politicians.

163

FERRERS

I have no intention of resigning.   Or of begging for time.   Either you trust me or you don't.   Meanwhile, I accept your order.

ADMIRAL
(*Surprised : looking from face to face*)
And these gentlemen—are they agreed ?

FERRERS

They will take my orders.

ADMIRAL

You make it easy, Ferrers.

FERRERS

That's as you see it, sir.

ADMIRAL

I haven't the least doubt in my own mind that by August 9—   I'm delighted that's settled—and much quicker than I could reasonably have expected. (*Endeavouring to be hearty*) I really needn't have turned my wife out at all. (*Goes and calls*) Sybil, dear. . . . It's all right, you can come back now.

LADY HELSTON
(*Re-appearing*)
Thank you, George.   You didn't keep me waiting very long after all.   I wish all your Service meetings were as abrupt.

ADMIRAL

Ferrers has smoothed everything out, by accepting the earlier date.

FERRERS

I have accepted an order.

LADY HELSTON

Can you carry it out?

FERRERS

There's one thing you can do for us, sir, if you would.

ADMIRAL

I'll do anything on earth.

FERRERS

We shall be working here, pretty well night and day. All leave will be stopped for men and officers. And we want to be left alone.

ADMIRAL

Quite—quite.

FERRERS

Will you issue an order, sir, that no one is to come here except strictly on duty by your written order or mine?

ADMIRAL

Certainly—I can quite understand the necessity——

LADY HELSTON

I understand too. It is deliberately aimed at me. (*To Ferrers*) Do you deny that?

FERRERS

(*makes no reply*)

LADY HELSTON

You ask my husband for an order to shut me out, and you ask for it in my presence.

FERRERS

You are here by your own choice.

LADY HELSTON

Do you think I want to come here ? (*She is now so angry and so unhappy that she cannot finish her sentences.*) Naturally I have taken an interest in the place. The rugs you are standing on are mine. The piano is mine. And when you found a girl coarse enough for your taste— Do you think I wanted her in my house ? She was quartered on me. I accepted even that.

ADMIRAL

Sybil, Miss Selby is our guest.

LADY HELSTON

She's not. Make no mistake about that. She *was*. She came slinking back to the house at all hours of the night and morning. You think I don't know what was going on ?

FERRERS

That's not true. Miss Selby——

LADY HELSTON

I don't want to hear about her. I'll have no more

of it. She can sleep where she likes and how she likes, but not in my house. You think that because you are an indispensable expert, you can do as you like. You will soon find out you can't. You've had your bluff called and you know it. Ask Mr. Sandford if he can be ready. (*To* SANDFORD) Can your detonator be ready? Can you re-pack your ridiculous trunk? (*To* FERRERS) Don't imagine you can treat me like this and get away with it. (*To* ADMIRAL) Do you mean to issue that order?

ADMIRAL

You had better go to the car.

LADY HELSTON

I asked you a question.

ADMIRAL

Mr Brissing, open the door.

LADY HELSTON

You mean that? Then give your own orders for Miss Selby's luggage to be moved where you please. (*Exit* LADY HELSTON.)

ADMIRAL

Miss Selby——

KAREN

Don't trouble about me, sir.

ADMIRAL

What shall you do?

KAREN

If I have permission, move here.

ADMIRAL

There are no other women here.   You would be—
afterwards, I mean—in the eyes of the world——

KAREN

I came here to work.

ADMIRAL

Look here, Miss Selby.   That house is my house——

KAREN

Let me come here, sir.

ADMIRAL

So be it.   (*At the door*) Get the job done, gentlemen.
Then women don't matter.   (*Exit* ADMIRAL, *followed by*
DENHAM.)

FERRERS

This evening we'll get out a new work schedule.
You'd better go back to the Power House, Carr.   (*To*
BRISSING) Can you get your bench test through before
the hands pack up for dinner?

BRISSING

The first part we can.   The rest later.   (CARR, BRIS-
SING *and* SANDFORD *move towards door*.)

168

CARR

Ferrers, why did you do that ?

FERRERS

What ?

CARR

Accept the early date.

FERRERS

We won't crawl to her. That's what she wants.
Poor old boy, he's in a worse fix than we are.

CARR

But if we're not ready—that's what she wants more.

FERRERS

We shall be—if you don't stand in doorways arguing.
... Dick, before you go, show me the spindle that's
worrying you. If we don't get that detonator right, we're
done. The charge won't go off. These people are like
children. If they don't see their puff of smoke, they'll
think the whole invention has failed. Show it to me.
I may get a line on it. (CARR *and* BRISSING *go out.*)

SANDFORD
(*Showing his drawing*)
It's this. Karen's idea is that if we shift the fulcrum
of 84 to point six-two from *that* end we get——

KAREN
(*Over their shoulders*)
You see, if the Scorpion inclines from the vertical

169

while the spindle is lifting, it's all right up to 38 degrees. After that—not. Where we've had detonator failures, the inclination has in fact been more than 38. There may be other causes too. Dick's trying to eliminate this one.

SANDFORD

But if you shift the fulcrum, you foul the compensating mechanism—and the compensating mechanism can't be shifted.

KAREN

That may be so unless——

FERRERS

Be quiet a minute, both of you. Dividers. (*Holds out his hand for them. Works with dividers on drawing.*) Slide rule. (*Works it.*) The odd thing is—we've tackled this problem before. You did, Karen.

KAREN

Never.

FERRERS

You did. I remember it now. Like a face. Every calculation has a face. You remember the expression of it even when you've forgotten the detail. You said we should have to fit a gyro—*here*. You began the gyro calculations.

KAREN

I didn't.

FERRERS

Not on this ?

170

KAREN

Never.

FERRERS

(*Remembering*)

It was your brother. Now I've got it. Go on, Dick, get down to your bench test. Karen and I will work on this. I don't know how far Selby took it but the beginning's there. Go on. Go on. (*He gets* SANDFORD *out of the room.*) This may be the answer to the whole damned thing. If it is, and if we can get it through in time, Dick's spindle mechanism can be cut out. That will cook her ladyship's goose.

KAREN

" If it is."

FERRERS

Well, find out. Your brother's stuff is still there.

KAREN

Any idea of its number ?

FERRERS

None. It's an early series. Probably B or C. We'll have to search the pigeon-holes. (*He is moving towards the Control Room but stops.*) Drink your tea first. You're tired. (*She hesitates—but she is tired, and sits down.*)

KAREN

You're tired, too. (*Puts out her hand to touch him. At once he moves away.*)

171   M

FERRERS

When this job's done——

KAREN

What shall you do then?

FERRERS

Do? Make my soul. It's about time. There's a devilish arrogance in doing things—if you do them well. Don't you feel it yourself? For instance, standing at that desk with Dick Sandford. He's as keen as a knife. He has one of the clearest and quickest mechanical minds I've ever known. He could construct anything from a torpedo to a lady's wrist-watch. *And* he gets a move on. But he keeps to the road. After the first mile, the second; after the second, the third; quick—but always on the road. He never jumps, he never flies; he doesn't —just *see*. I do. And you do. Don't you feel sometimes like an eagle taking a chicken for a walk?

KAREN

I suppose so.

FERRERS

And we call that genius. Anyhow, we let other people call it genius for us. It's not, you know. Not the genius that matters, anyway. In itself, the genius of action and intellect isn't much more than a trick. It's a damnable false pride. I have no illusions about the job we're doing here. If it comes off, we shall be told we have saved the world. I shall be invited to dine by the war-lords one evening and by the pacifists the next. But all we shall have done is to make the air unsafe for bombers. Large numbers of people will live a few years longer. I doubt if that's a service to the world if they don't know how to live at all.

KAREN

You haven't talked to me of anything—except the job—for months. Why do you now?

FERRERS

Because I'm tired and you are—and we have to go on one month longer, the worst of all. And because, in the end, this thing may seem to have failed.

KAREN

But why to-day, suddenly? You were on your way to the Control Room. Then you stopped and changed —as if you were a human being. Why now?

FERRERS

Was I wrong?

KAREN

So desperately right. . . . Did you know?

FERRERS

I knew I was losing you.

KAREN

I was losing myself.

173

FERRERS

How unhappy are you, Karen ?

KAREN

If I could put a circle round any instant of time and keep it always, I'd choose this. . . . It's strange.   We've struggled so long not to talk in this way—and now we do—and it's—safe and—oh, it's not !   It's not !   (*He has taken both her hands.*)

FERRERS

Let it be unsafe, Karen.   Once.   It may never come again.   Put a circle round this moment too.   (FERRERS *is drawing her to him, but she does not yield.*)

FERRERS

Why do you say no ?

KAREN

Not now.   Not yet.   It would blind us.   (*He lets her go.   Beneath this impact, they talk as much to themselves as to each other.*)

FERRERS

Then——

KAREN
(*Her hand across her eyes*)

It's true.   I can scarcely see you.

FERRERS
(*Holding out his empty hands*)

I still have the weight of your hands. . . . How cool they are.

KAREN

What time is it ?

FERRERS
(*He is by* SANDFORD's *desk*)
Here's the slide-rule where I put it down.

KAREN

What made you order this tea for me ?

FERRERS

I think I did.

KAREN

Ages ago.   (*Silence.*)

FERRERS

Now I can work.

KAREN

Yes.

FERRERS
(*Taking out his key*)
Come and open.   (*She rises and puts her hand inside her dress for the key she carries on a chain round her neck.*)

KAREN

I haven't got it.

FERRERS

What ?

KAREN

I haven't the key.

175

FERRERS

Where is it? You were never to let that key out of your possession.

KAREN

I don't. I carry it always—on a chain—round my neck.

FERRERS

Well?

KAREN

I'm sorry. . . . Why are you so angry? It's not lost. It's at the house. I'd been working all night. I was half-asleep when I dressed this morning. I forgot to put it on—that's all. Why are you so angry? You frighten me.

FERRERS

Do you remember taking it off? Why do you take it off at all?

KAREN

I put it on again before I sleep—always.

FERRERS

Did you, this time?

KAREN

I don't remember.

FERRERS

Do you remember anything?

KAREN

I was dead beat. Don't you understand? Why does it matter so much? You have only to send for it.

FERRERS

Now we can do nothing. I'm shut out of my own Control Room. We can do nothing, nothing all day until your damnable carelessness is made good.

KAREN

If you sent a messenger in the car——

FERRERS
(*Takes hold of her*)
Will you stop talking? Stop. Stop.

KAREN

Your hands! You are hurting!

FERRERS
(*Letting her go violently*)
I wish to God you weren't a woman. Because you are I can do nothing. You can do this and you can stand there and say you're sorry. I can do nothing to you. It's like being bound with cords. It's like being divided from you by a wall of glass. Get out of the room. Out of my reach. Out of my reach.

KAREN

You can do what you like.

177

FERRERS

Come here.   Let me look at you.   Inside you, what are you thinking?

KAREN

Of your suffering.

FERRERS

You are not thinking at all about the key.

KAREN

It's of no importance.   Nor what you do to me. Nor what I have done.

FERRERS

(*Coming out of a dream*)

None. . . . This is one of the episodes in our lives we shall both forget.   We shall seem to remember it.

KAREN

I shall say: " Do you remember the day when you could have beaten me because I had forgotten the key? " And you will answer : " I remember."

FERRERS

But we shan't recognize ourselves in the remembrance.

KAREN

I think that must be true of murderers—they don't recognize themselves in the remembrance.

FERRERS

If I had struck you then—to the world the blow would have been everything—and to you?

KAREN

Whatever it was to you—not more or less. (*Enter* BRISSING.)

BRISSING

The Admiral's coxswain brought up this key. Found on your dressing-table, Karen.

KAREN

Thank you. . . . (*Calling him back*) Peter !

BRISSING

What ?

KAREN

There will be no answer.

BRISSING

No answer ?

KAREN

To the question you asked. There can be no answer. There could never have been. Do you understand ?

BRISSING

Yes. . . . I see. . . . I'll be getting back. (*Exit* BRISSING.)

FERRERS

What question was that ?

KAREN

Something he and I got muddled about. It doesn't arise now.

179

FERRERS

(*As they begin to move towards Control Room, laughing*)
For God's sake put that key round your neck and keep
it there.

KAREN

When this is over, will you give it me ?

FERRERS

That depends.

KAREN

On what ?

FERRERS

Listen.   Let's get this straight.   We love each other.
Is that true ?

KAREN

I love you.

FERRERS

But if this job goes wrong, we shall never marry.   (*He
waits for her answer but gets none.*)   Do you understand
that ?

KAREN

No.

FERRERS

Then you don't understand me. . . . And, my God,
you don't understand yourself.   How long are you going
to want a man you despise ?

KAREN

Despise.

FERRERS

Pity, then. Have you ever been maternal towards anyone you loved ? Anyhow, I don't want it—not from you. I'm a god to you or nothing. I know that. If this job crashes, I'll pay someone else to wheel my bath-chair.

KAREN

I thought *I* was arrogant—but you frighten me.

FERRERS

That's why you love me.

KAREN

(*Looking at him for a long moment*)
Is that why ?

FERRERS

Isn't it ? Anyhow, it's one of six reasons why I love you. Does that make the arrogance worse ?

KAREN

What are the other five ?

FERRERS

My dear, if the trial succeeds, I will prove the other five. Then you shall have your key, if you'll take it.

KAREN

(*Steadily, deliberately*)
And if we fail.

FERRERS

No, my Karen, if this thing fails, that's an end for us.
Let's believe it won't fail. Come and unlock.

Curtain

ACT II

SCENE 2

Five weeks later. 5 o'clock, August 16. The big table is littered with the papers of an interrupted conference. Chairs are set near it. The room looks untidy, used and stale, for the conference has been going on all the afternoon. BRISSING *alone on sofa, bored and kicking his heels. Rises, empties ash-trays into waste-paper basket, and piles them on piano. Picks up papers from floor.*

BRISSING
(*Singing*)

" As far as I know
   It's the end of the show
      And now we go home to bed—to bed
      And now we go home to——"

(*Telephone rings. Goes to it.*) Yes. Block House. Brissing speaking. Oh, yes. You bet he's still here— and the Admiral. The inquiry's still going on. Having a tea interval. Well, it's damned irregular. Do you usually distribute signals by wardroom telephone ? . . . Don't be a fool, Flags. Of course I'll take it. Hold on. I haven't a pad. (*Fetches signal pad and pencil. Sits to write.*) Carry on. Dictate . . . P.M.O. Hospital, Kendrickstown to Flag. Regret report Murphy died 4.23." I'll read back. (*Repeats casually at high speed*) O.K. ? . . . What ? Oh, they've been going over the same ground all the afternoon. The Admiral's trying to be judicial. I don't believe he'll close down on us. But the Flag-Captain's dead against us. He's a clever swine. He baits Ferrers. That makes it worse. One thing about it, if they pack us up, it means a spot of leave. . . . All right. (*Rings off. Goes towards mess-room door, signal pad in hand.* KAREN *enters, walks past him in silence.*) What are the chances, Karen ?

KAREN

They go for facts. The trial failed—anyhow they think it did. I said what I could.

BRISSING
(*Admiring*)

You did your bit—like hell ! The Admiral lapped it up !

KAREN

He wanted to, I think. But it needs courage if the Admiralty expects him to report against us.

BRISSING

Are you sure they do ?

KAREN

Wedgcroft will be against us. How much ice does he cut ?

BRISSING

He's not all the Admiralty, though he is Lady Helston's brother.

KAREN

Edward says the Treasury is through. They want results. All they get is eight Scorpions that didn't explode their blank charge *and* a crashed aeroplane *and* the observer dead.

BRISSING
(*Holding out pad*)

The pilot too. Murphy died in hospital half an hour ago.

KAREN
(*Having looked at it*)

That doesn't make it easier.

BRISSING

The Flag Captain will make the most of it.

KAREN

Oh, Peter, if they do close us down, it will kill *him*.

BRISSING

Ferrers.

KAREN
(*To herself*)

The principle isn't affected by the detonator failures.

185

Why can't they see ? I think the Admiral does see—in his heart.

BRISSING

That Ferrers is right ? But if the Admiral sees that, he *can't* close us down.

KAREN

Can't he ? I believe I know him better than you. He's not a coward and he's not dishonest and he's not really convinced. It needs guts to be convinced of anything—and stick to it. In the past, men on the spot had full powers. They were expected to use their imagination. Whitehall let them be. Now, speed of communications has made every kind of mess of the world. It has taken the heart out of all but the greatest men. You have to be a lion not to be led on a string. The Admiral's not a lion. He's an affable dog who knows his master's voice. He'll begin to say to himself : " Well, I dunno. P'raps I'm wrong." That's what he'd like Edward to say : " Well, I dunno. P'raps I *am* wrong." It's a polite habit. Modest. Charming. . . . Damnable.

BRISSING
(*Shy, consoling*)

I hate this—for you. If things go wrong, for me it's different. First I get leave—London. I shall see her. Then Guns in a Home Fleet cruiser.

KAREN
(*Coming out of her own trouble*)

You heard from her last mail ?

BRISSING

How did you know?

KAREN

Because you didn't tell me.

BRISSING

I see. . . . I'm sorry. I'm afraid I have poured out my heart a bit. I suppose I'm damned young still. (*Portentously*) She's older than I am, you know.

KAREN
(*Smiling*)

You didn't confess that. Much?

BRISSING

Nearly two years.

KAREN

Grey?

BRISSING

(*Laughs. Takes her hand affectionately. Kisses it*)
Bless you. You'd be good with puppies.

KAREN
(*Vehement*)

What did you say?

BRISSING
(*Taken aback*)

I said—you'd be good with puppies. Why? . . . I'm sorry if—I only meant you'd been good to me.

187   N

KAREN

You've repaid it.

BRISSING

How?

KAREN

By saying that. . . . You'll go to London——

BRISSING

We'll meet.

KAREN

(*Keyed up*)

Of course.   You'll ask me to lunch and tell me about her.   After a bit we shall meet again.   You'll tell me about your children.   Don't forget to ask me.

BRISSING

Karen, what's wrong?

KAREN

I shan't forget ever.   The man who said—to-day of all days—I should be good with puppies.

BRISSING

My dear——

KAREN

It's all right.   (*She goes up to him and kisses him.*) What about that signal?

BRISSING

They're coming out.   (*Enter* ADMIRAL, FLAG CAPTAIN, FERRERS, SANDFORD *and* CARR.)

ADMIRAL

The tea wasn't as good after you'd gone, Miss Selby.

KAREN

I'm sorry, sir.

BRISSING
(*To* FLAG CAPTAIN, *presenting signal*)
Relayed from Flag, sir.

FLAG CAPTAIN
(*To* ADMIRAL)
Young Murphy's dead, sir.   Died 4.23. . . . Relayed from Flag.   (*Presents signal.*)

ADMIRAL

I see.   Do we know anything about him ?   People and so on ?   Not a married man ?

FLAG CAPTAIN

No, single.

ADMIRAL

Good. . . . Well, we'd better get on.   Are you ready, Ferrers ?

FERRERS

Yes, sir.   But there's no need to take up more of your

189

time, sir. Miss Selby has put my case very clearly. Clear to me, anyhow. I have nothing fresh to add.

ADMIRAL

But I have more to ask. I want no regrets.

FERRERS

I understand that, sir.

FLAG CAPTAIN

Sarcasm does no good, Ferrers.

ADMIRAL
(*Smoothing over*)

Was that sarcasm?

FLAG CAPTAIN

Ferrers said, sir, that——

ADMIRAL

Never mind. I didn't hear it. Now, let's get on. (*Sits at table.*) Men get tired, you know. (*But he is on edge himself and shouts at* CARR *who is wandering about the room*) Sit, Carr. Don't wander about like a dog that's lost its tail. (CARR *sits in the chair that happens to be nearest to him. The* ADMIRAL *is at the table with the* FLAG CAPTAIN *on his right, and* FERRERS *in a chair nearby from which he can face them both.*)

FLAG CAPTAIN
(*To* BRISSING)

Ash-trays.

BRISSING

What, sir ?

FLAG CAPTAIN

What the devil have you done with the ash-trays ?

BRISSING

Emptied them.

FLAG CAPTAIN

Well, where are they ? (BRISSING *collects the pile from piano, and distributes them. Meanwhile*—)

ADMIRAL

Now then.

FLAG CAPTAIN

Before we begin I should like to say one or two words, sir, entirely in Ferrers' own interest. I feel that his attitude throughout the afternoon has been most unhelpful. I hope——

ADMIRAL

I expect a dish of tea has done all our tempers good. Admirable tea, Miss Selby. Nothing like making it oneself.

FERRERS

(*Angry*)

In any case, what is this ? A court-martial ?

FLAG CAPTAIN

Certainly not, but it remains true——

191

FERRERS

Then I don't want a prisoner's friend.

FLAG CAPTAIN

You will please not interrupt me when I am speaking.

FERRERS
(*Unrepentantly*)

I apologize.

ADMIRAL
(*Affably amused, to* BRISSING, *who is still slowly
distributing ash-trays*)

Well, have you finished?

BRISSING

Yes, sir.

ADMIRAL

Quite finished? Every ash-tray in its place?

BRISSING

Yes, sir.

FLAG CAPTAIN
(*Irritable*)

Well, sit down and keep quiet, young man. Now,
Ferrers. (*Seeing* CARR *standing up at back of room*) Well,
what is it?

CARR

Nothing, sir. (*Sits down again.*)

ADMIRAL

Yes, Carr. I should like to hear you.

CARR

It's this, sir. Ferrers is up against it in a very special way. I speak a bit of his language—enough to see the difficulties—but the truth is that none of us understands it. Except Miss Selby.

FLAG CAPTAIN

Then he might take the trouble to learn ours.

KAREN

You wouldn't ask a musician to learn ours.

FLAG CAPTAIN

And why not ? Don't they talk like ordinary people when they're not playing their music ? Except that most of them seem to be Poles—or mad.

KAREN

Yes, sir, but that's different. What they say in words isn't what they say in music. If it were, there'd be no need of the music.

FERRERS

The Flag Captain isn't interested in music, Karen.

ADMIRAL

(*To* CARR)

You were saying—" in *his* language ", Carr ?

193

CARR

The language of mathematics, sir.

ADMIRAL

I see.   Still, we must do the best we can to meet each
other half-way.   Eh, Miss Selby?

KAREN

I know, sir.   But sometimes there isn't any half-way.
Just as there isn't really any half-way between a music-
hall song and Beethoven's Fifth.

ADMIRAL

Now, gentlemen, I must write my report this evening.
Since the trial we have spent a week—your own officers,
Ferrers, and independent officers from the Fleet—in-
vestigating the causes of failure.   We have had their
reports.   To-day we have heard their evidence.

FERRERS

I don't admit failure, sir.

ADMIRAL

That's one of the difficulties.   It would be simpler if
you did.

FERRERS

I admit that the detonators——

ADMIRAL

One minute, please.   You will have your chance.
First, I don't want to misrepresent you.   I will go over

194

the facts as I shall report them. You can check as I go. Now, Ferrers. Follow my notes. If I'm wrong, stop me. Murphy and Gaisford took up their aeroplane. As soon as you located them, you launched your first Scorpion. It followed them in the air. (FLAG CAPTAIN *yawns and fidgets*.)

FERRERS

Will you make that point, sir? It *did* follow them. It followed them close.

CARR

It passed very close, sir. They nose-dived to avoid it.

ADMIRAL

I accept that. But when close, the vibrations of the plane ought to have fired the charge. Isn't that so? In war, high explosive that would bring the plane down. In this case a blank charge that should have given off a puff of smoke. Is that right, Ferrers?

FERRERS

Yes, sir.

ADMIRAL

But there was no puff of smoke. That means you failed to fire the charge at the appropriate moment. The Scorpion lost power and fell.

FERRERS

The facts are right. Not your conclusions from them.

ADMIRAL

But there are seven more facts.   Murphy and Gaisford began a second run.   You launched a second Scorpion. Again it followed them.   This time it hit them, brought them down—with what results we know.

FERRERS

It proves at any rate that the Scorpion followed them.

FLAG CAPTAIN

That's brutal and callous.

FERRERS

It proves the vibration-steering worked.

ADMIRAL

The Scorpion ought to have exploded.   It didn't explode.   Isn't that a second failure ?

FERRERS

You can put it so.

FLAG CAPTAIN

And there's this point.   You saw Murphy and Gaisford crash into the sea.   Even then you didn't break off your mad series of failures.

FERRERS

The destroyers were under them.   There was nothing I could do.

FLAG CAPTAIN

You don't seem to care how many you kill. But Whitehall will care. You must be stopped.

FERRERS

If I had stopped then, you would have said I had failed. I ordered another plane up.

FLAG CAPTAIN

Do they matter so little, these poor men? You can count Miss Selby's brother with them.

FERRERS
(*Furious*)

I know that. I was his friend. What does he or any of us matter if the thing is right?

FLAG CAPTAIN

You must be mad, Ferrers. You couldn't speak in that way.

ADMIRAL
(*To* FERRERS)

You make it hard. Still—there's little more. Are these the remaining facts? You sent up another aeroplane. This time we have the observers' reports. They did six more runs. You launched six Scorpions——

FERRERS

And each time followed them in the air.

197

ADMIRAL

But you didn't explode.

FERRERS

I followed them close.   The observer reports that.

ADMIRAL

But failed to explode.

FERRERS

Yes.

ADMIRAL

Six times.

FERRERS

Yes.

ADMIRAL

Eight in all.

FERRERS

Eight in all.

ADMIRAL

Is there any answer to that ?

KAREN

Sandford and I gave the answer in great detail this morning, sir.   The detonators didn't work.

FLAG CAPTAIN

Eight times ?

198

SANDFORD

They are all positioned the same. If one is wrong, they all are.

FLAG CAPTAIN

You say the detonators. And yet you say the invention is not affected in principle. Now, listen to me, Ferrers. What causes, or should cause, your detonator to fire the charge?

FERRERS

Air vibration on sensitive receivers.

FLAG CAPTAIN

Exactly! And vibration is the root of your theory, isn't it?

SANDFORD

I should like to say, sir——

FLAG CAPTAIN

Be quiet, Mr. Sandford. (*To* FERRERS) Isn't vibration the root of your theory?

FERRERS

Certainly it is.

FLAG CAPTAIN

Vibration should explode your detonators?

FERRERS

Yes.

FLAG CAPTAIN

And the detonators failed to explode?

199

FERRERS

Yes.

FLAG CAPTAIN

Then your whole theory breaks down !

FERRERS

No. The receivers are not yet rightly placed. Would it have proved that Watt was a fool if the lid of the kettle had stuck ?

ADMIRAL

There's no proof that the fault was in the detonator receivers. There can be none. Such Scorpions as we recovered were too much damaged. The independent officers simply say they don't know. Sandford says——

SANDFORD

Damn it, sir, I made the thing. It's my child.

ADMIRAL

A mother isn't always the best judge of her own child.

KAREN

That wasn't Solomon's opinion, sir. (*They laugh. It is a relief.*)

ADMIRAL

Thank you, Miss Selby, we needed that. You say there was a detonator fault, Sandford. What was it ?

(SANDFORD *hesitates.*) Come, that, surely, is a fair question.

SANDFORD

Sounds like it, I know, sir. I'll never be able to convince you that it isn't. Our trouble at the end was simply how to place the detonator mechanism. When the difficulty arose, I had to repack the whole inside of the torpedo. Meanwhile, Ferrers was working on a new gyro-gear which would save space. Our time was cut down from two months to one. The tests were rushed through. I knew we were taking a chance. It's a thousand to one that the fault is still the effect of screening on the detonator receivers.

ADMIRAL

That's too vague, Sandford. Can't you go further?

SANDFORD

Not now, sir, I can't.

ADMIRAL

It may be vital.

SANDFORD
(*Desperate*)

I can't, sir. I— (*But there is nothing more he can say.*)

ADMIRAL

That's the end then.

201

KAREN

Give us time, sir. It's *so* near. We can re-position the existing detonator mechanism. Or we can work out the alternative. Then the thing will prove itself.

ADMIRAL

We can't go on indefinitely without results. Listen, Ferrers, you may be right. (FERRERS *stands and faces him. After a moment,* KAREN *also stands.*) I may be looking now at the man who has it in his power to make Great Britain an island again. If I report against you, this station will be closed down. This isn't work you can do without government backing. I may be breaking the one man who might save civilization. To avoid that, I will take great risks. I came here prepared, against the evidence, to advise further experiment, if you frankly admitted an error in your own calculations and were prepared to correct it. (*Waits.*) Well, Ferrers? (*Silence.*)

FLAG CAPTAIN

There's no more to say, sir.

ADMIRAL

I want the Commander's answer. (KAREN *moves towards* FERRERS. CARR *and* BRISSING *stand.*) Are you willing to reconsider your formula from first principles?

FERRERS

No, sir. I'm not being stubborn. If I do, calculation simply stops. It's like denying that twice two make four. You can deny it in words, but, if you do,

you can't go on. It's not modesty and sweet reason to
deny it. It's barren folly.

ADMIRAL

Then you won't go back ?

FERRERS

I can't, sir.

FLAG CAPTAIN

If we did give you more time—more money, more
lives to throw away—who would be responsible next
time you failed ? (*With venom*) I can tell you. One of
your staff, Ferrers. Sandford again, or Carr or Brissing.
Perhaps even Miss Selby by that time. Anyone but you.

FERRERS

You can think that if you like. I can't lie about my
own work. (*Sits down, worn out.*)

ADMIRAL

Doesn't it occur to you—even as a possibility—that
you may *be* wrong ?

FERRERS

(*Quietly*)

I'm as sure of this as I am of the existence of God.

FLAG CAPTAIN

I believe you're mad, Ferrers.

FERRERS

That's a feather in my cap.

FLAG CAPTAIN

And if it were proved that your calculation was wrong —what then ?

FERRERS

(*Springs up*)

When it is proved to me that my truth is my lie, then for me all truth is lying and I am mad.

KAREN

(*To* ADMIRAL)

I know that he is right.

FLAG CAPTAIN

Well, sir ?

ADMIRAL

(*After a long pause*)

I wash my hands of it.

KAREN

I know deep down.   I do know.

ADMIRAL

Other men have believed in themselves, Miss Selby. Other women have believed in them.   I don't blame you.   Good-bye, Ferrers.   (ADMIRAL *and* FLAG CAPTAIN *go out, all standing as they go, even* FERRERS *on his feet. Afterwards there is a long silence.* CARR *is at the piano.*)

SANDFORD

Well, what's the good of sitting on a music-stool?

CARR

(*Rises from piano*)

Sybil Helston will have a good evening. Play piquet, Dick. That table's a shambles. Come to the mess-room. (CARR *and* SANDFORD *go out.*)

BRISSING

Karen, make it four and bridge. Oh, you don't play. Five and poker. (*No answer.*) Hell, I'll play Miss Milligan. (*Exit* BRISSING.)

FERRERS

What's the time?

KAREN

Six-eight.

FERRERS

Still accurate. As if there were work to do.

KAREN

There still is.

FERRERS

Not for me.

KAREN

This particular invention isn't everything.

205

FERRERS

What do you mean ?   Pluck up courage and make something else in the service of mankind ?   What—an electrical bicycle ?

KAREN

If you never invent anything that people manufacture and use, it doesn't matter to you—any more than it matters to a poet whether the world decides he's morally helpful.   Mathematics is a thing of its own.   Absolute.

FERRERS

But one must exercise it on something.   There must be a theme.

KAREN

Before I came here, much of my work was useful—anyhow to astronomers—to navigators, too, remotely. But much of it was quite useless.   What it came down to was discovering the natural laws of an imaginary universe.   I was happy—using myself.   Dead single-minded.

FERRERS

I've been happy in this place.   You're good to work with.

KAREN

Oh——

FERRERS

What ?

KAREN

I was thinking of something Brissing said while you were at tea.

FERRERS

What did he say?

KAREN

Something about—dogs.

FERRERS

Dogs?

KAREN

Well, about—oh, never mind that. I'm good to work with. I meant to be.

FERRERS

You'll go home.

KAREN

Let me wait and clear up. If I were a man I should.

FERRERS

You're not.

KAREN

You said, long ago, you would treat me as a man. Now I claim it.

FERRERS

They'll cut down the salary list. You're supernumerary.

KAREN

I know.

FERRERS

Why, in God's name, are we talking like this?

KAREN

Because we're still afraid of each other.

FERRERS

We were right to be afraid.

KAREN

While there was work to spoil. There's only one real misery in life—to be entangled.

FERRERS
(*An outburst*)

You don't know what I've had from women!

KAREN

I can guess.

FERRERS

Open a door—and be damned if they'll walk in. Shut it, bolt it and they'll *break* in. And once in, it's for ever and ever, unless *they* want to go out again. Then it's " Good-bye, my lady. I am honoured to have served your turn. Please allow me to be eternally your friend and pay the damage for the next lock you break . . ."

KAREN

I see.

FERRERS

You have been honest, Karen. Always, with me. From the beginning of your life, I think. If you were a tart, you'd be an honest tart. There was a girl kept a bar once. In fact she wasn't a tart—men fell in love with her. They proposed marriage and meant it. Half the young bloods in the Service—peerage, money, brains—she could have put a dozen careers in her pocket. But she wouldn't. Even when she herself loved one of them —still she wouldn't. My God, I admire that woman. She may have had fifty lovers. I don't think she did. She may have. It makes no odds. What she said, you believed. Honest—like you.

KAREN

Honest. Good to work with. Good with puppies. Respectable virtues.

FERRERS

Puppies ?

KAREN

That's what Brissing said.

FERRERS

Ring for a drink. (*She moves.*) Karen ! (*She turns back.*) I see everything ahead like a blank wall. (*She is behind him and nearly takes him in her arms, but holds back.*) Come and sit here again. I want to say something. Just for the satisfaction of having once said it, I suppose. That first day, in this room, do you remember we were by the table ? I sat down and left you standing ? Do you know what I saw ?

KAREN

A junior officer being interviewed.

FERRERS

No. A woman—naked. I want you to know. That and— (*A long pause.*) Oh, it *is* true that one thinks and feels and wants two things at the same time. People who write won't allow that. They arrange the emotions in order—first a man doesn't desire a woman, then he does, then desire grows, as they say, to " something more "—it's all beautifully ordered, everything in its sequence. It's all a lie. The emotions aren't a reasonable sequence. At the same time, I saw you as— oh, something to eat, and behind that, like a fate, as something to worship. At one and the same time ! And I said : " She'll break up this work ; she's hell ; she'll play her own game." And at the same time I knew : " She's the Holy Grail." . . . Well, that's said.

KAREN

That was honest, too.

FERRERS

If to-day hadn't gone as it did. . . . I'll tell you that, too. If it hadn't, I mean if we had been going on working here, I should have taken you if I could.

KAREN

My dear, I am all yours.

FERRERS

Not now.

KAREN

Always, without terms.   From the beginning, to the end, without terms, yours absolutely.

FERRERS

I'm broke, my Karen.

KAREN

(*Sharply—angry*)

Broke ?

FERRERS

I don't mean money.   I'm a broke man.

KAREN

All the more——

FERRERS

(*Resenting pity*)

All the more !

KAREN

(*Trying to recover*)

Not " all the more "—the same, absolutely.

FERRERS

Too late, Karen.

KAREN

You think I'm pitying you !   I—you !   Why are you so afraid of hurting, I wonder.

FERRERS

Because I know myself.   I hurt too much.

KAREN

Afraid of believing, too.

FERRERS

I have believed too much.

KAREN

Believe now.   (*Her arms about him.*)   Believe now.

FERRERS

(*Takes her passionately.   Then, in bitter reaction, but
still holding her*)
You know what would happen ?

KAREN

What would happen ?

FERRERS

The man you love was proud as Lucifer.   Possessed
by your own devil of genius.   That's the kind goes phut.
Not if I was twenty-five.   But as things are, we should
drift about Swiss Cottage in gallant poverty.   You'd
work in your Observatory and keep me.   Or you'd get
me a job there and we'd promote ourselves to Kensington.
People would say " Wasn't your husband a mathematical
genius ? "   Someone would give me a teaching job—
I'd fly out and lose it—and, my God, you'd endure that,
again—and again—and again.   As I grew older, I should

get the smug pride of the genius who's missed it—the little man whose poetry the world is always too stupid to read or whose music is too exalted for anyone to listen to.

KAREN

(*Trying to break free*)

Oh, stop ! You're cruel.

FERRERS

No. Stay in my arms while you hear it. Then you'll know. You'd be in my arms then. Month after month, year after year. Night after night.

KAREN

Happy—happy—happy with each other.

FERRERS

Not if I hated myself. Then I should hate you. And I should hate myself all right. We shouldn't dare speak of Kendrickstown. Happy—with you !—you're the one woman above all others who would drive me mad.

KAREN

Because I love you ?

FERRERS

Because you had my own faith in me. You thought —didn't you ?—I was going to save the world ? You'd see the world-shaker come home every evening with his latch-key. " Well, my dear, did you have a good day at the office ? " Oh no. If any woman's going to wake on my pillow, it must be one who doesn't know. I could say to her : " Yes. For about three years I tried some experiments under the Admiralty. They were extraordinarily interesting at the time." She'd believe me. She'd be proud of my bridge. " That's what comes," she'd say, when we added up the score, " that's what comes of having been a mathematical genius." She——

KAREN

Let me go, then.

FERRERS

Kiss me. (*Violently.*)

KAREN

Oh my God !

FERRERS

(*Kisses her again*)
Now I'll remember.

KAREN

What ?

FERRERS

This too. And when she says—oh whatever she says—I'll feel that ribbon, across your shoulder, under your dress—now. (*Drops her.*) Shall I ever feel it ? Or just forget.

KAREN

Do something for me. Be still. Quite still. I want you here. (*Draws him down.*) I love you, always, without terms, as I know you love me. I shall try to

remember too.   But it's the chance things one remembers.
My father tying a balloon for me.   It was a piece of red
wool.   I suppose I shall forget this—it will go vague.
(*Trying to plant them in her memory*.) I shall say : " The
lamp.   His fingers on my flesh.   The weight of his head."
I shall remember.   But I shan't *feel* the weight of your
head.   O my beloved, can you believe in only one
absolute thing ?   There is an absolute love.   They are
the same, I think. (*He moves*.)   A little longer.   Be
still and remember.   We love each other always—
through all follies, all unfaithfulness—through every
failure and denial—*all parting*—always—to the end.

FERRERS
Karen, that's the hope of madmen.

KAREN
So is the love of God.

Curtain

ACT III

ACT III

*Two months later. 3 P.M. Very hot. Dress: full
whites. Signs of dismantling. Packing cases. Some of
the pictures gone from the walls.* CARR *is on piano-stool,
idly strumming.* SANDFORD *walking up and down room as
if it were a cage.* BRISSING, *on his knees, is hammering a
packing case. They are all ill-tempered and on edge—the
spirit gone out of them. Except* CARR, *they have drunk
enough. The tune* CARR *plays is " Farewell and Adieu ".
He uses it throughout the opening of this scene, quietly or
loudly, as a counter to the nerves of others—as a nurse uses
a song to lull fractious children, at last tempting them to
join in.*

BRISSING
(Stops hammering)
You can say what you like. The First Lord wouldn't
have come from England again without a reason.

CARR
It wasn't to save this place.

BRISSING
I'm not so sure. This morning he was out to listen.
So was the Admiral at the inquiry two months ago.
Twice Ferrers' damned obstinacy has chucked the game
away. (KAREN *drifts in from verandah and lies on sofa*

*down stage, turning over illustrated papers.   They take no
notice of her.)*

SANDFORD
(*To* BRISSING)

Not so loyal now !

BRISSING

It was you let him down over the detonator.   (*Echoing* ADMIRAL.)   " What was the defect ?   Surely that's
a fair question, Mr. Sandford ? "   You hadn't a damned
thing to say.   (*Begins to hammer again.*)

CARR

Dry up, Brissing.

BRISSING

Why should I ?   We've got to pack.   (*Hammers.*)

CARR
(*A calm man now at breaking-point.   Almost a cry
of agony*)

No, no !   Stop !

BRISSING

Sensitive ?   Do you mind, Karen ?

CARR
(*With real entreaty*)

I can't stand the noise.   I don't know why.   (*As*
BRISSING *continues to hammer,* CARR *turns again to the
piano.   He plays and sings his loudest.   One by one,
the others join in—a jangled, unprofessional chorus.   One*

by one, they stop, but the piano continues, and one of them—
KAREN *perhaps—takes the last lines alone.* Silence. CARR
*transposes a few bars into G minor. They are appeased
and surprised by their appeasement.*)

BRISSING
(*To* CARR)
Sorry I was a fool. . . . Cut for drinks.

SANDFORD

I will.

BRISSING

Karen, you coming in ?

KAREN

If you bring the dice over to me. (*They throw dice on
a table within her reach.*) Sybil Helston's coming here.

SANDFORD

What for ?

KAREN

She telephoned a message asking if she could. She's
going to England in the First Lord's ship to-morrow.

BRISSING

Do you mean, a farewell call on the Mess ? It's not
possible.

KAREN

She wants to see me.

BRISSING

You're going to ?

KAREN

Yes.   (*The dice-throwing is now over.*)

BRISSING

(*Who has thrown last*)

Four straight aces. Good enough ? You're lurked,
Sandford.   (SANDFORD *rings bell.*)

CARR

Does Ferrers know she's coming ?

KAREN

I asked his permission.

SANDFORD

Women beat me.   Why didn't you refuse to see her ?

KAREN

I don't believe in refusing to see people.   You wonder
afterwards what they had to say.   (*Enter* DENHAM.)

SANDFORD

Two whiskies.   What for you, Karen ?

KAREN

I don't want one.

SANDFORD

But you came in.

KAREN

Still, I don't.

222

SANDFORD

(*To* DENHAM)

All right, two then.

KAREN

Denham, Lady Helston is coming to see me. Show her straight in when she comes.

DENHAM

Very good, Miss. (*Exit.*)

KAREN

Can I have this room ?

CARR

Why not the mess-room ? This is like a carpenter's shop.

KAREN

I think this would be good for her.

BRISSING

We'll clear out the packing-case. (*To* SANDFORD) Give me a hand. (*They carry it out.*)

KAREN

(*To* CARR)

Don't go for a minute.

CARR

I don't see what good it can do—her coming here.

KAREN

It's not that I want to talk to you about. (BRISSING

returns to pick up hammer, etc. KAREN *is turning over illustrated papers again.*)

BRISSING

That's hopelessly stale. Lord Coverdale has been dining at the Savoy with the charming wife of Mr. Lionel P. Soot of Boston, Mass., for the last six weeks. (*Enter* DENHAM *with drinks.*) Take them through to Mr. Sandford. Give me mine on the way. (*Exit* DENHAM. BRISSING *offers another paper to* KAREN.) Try this one. There's a whole page of the people who found the photographer on Mr. Cochran's first night. The civilization we have failed to save . . .

> . . . Holy People's will—
> Have no truck with the senseless thing.
> Order the guns and kill !

Sorry, I must still be sober. I'll remedy that defect. (*Exit* BRISSING *with drink.*)

KAREN

Sit for a moment. (CARR *perches himself on the arm of her sofa.*)

KAREN

This is very like hell.

CARR

My dear—as bad as that ?

KAREN

Those two are drinking a lot of drink.

CARR

Naval officers can drink a lot of drink.

KAREN

You are the only one who isn't rattled.

CARR

You *will* go on hoping. I write things off.

KAREN

Like Antony? " Things that are past are done with me." They are done with him too.

CARR

Ferrers.

KAREN

He's not fighting any more. When I heard the First Lord was coming out from England, I thought there was still a chance.

CARR

Politicians aren't gods from the machine.

KAREN

If he didn't mean to do anything but back the Admiral, why come?

CARR

To square his own yard arm. A lot of money has been spent in this place. Three lives too, and the Admiralty has nothing to show for it. There'll be questions. Harrowby will have to tell discreet lies or square the Opposition. He can tell 'em better if he can say he's been here.

KAREN

I see. Just that.

CARR

I think so.

KAREN

(*After a pause*)

Do you believe in him ?

CARR

The First Lord ?

KAREN

In Edward. The others have begun to shake.

CARR

Brissing and Dick Sandford ? You know why ?

KAREN

That's what I want to know.

CARR

I see their point of view. If Ferrers had eaten a bit of humble pie and admitted he was wrong, the Admiral would have given him more time.

KAREN

Would have ? Not now ?

CARR

Now ? It's too late. We're for home in a fortnight. Didn't you hear Brissing nailing down the coffin ? . . .

What he and Dick say is : If Ferrers really knows that he's right, why the hell didn't he go through the motions of putting his pride in his pocket ? We aren't Christian martyrs refusing a pinch of incense to the altar of Caesar.

KAREN

So they think he ought to lie about his own work ?

CARR

They say : If the job is everything to him, wouldn't he lie to save it—unless he really *is* wrong and doesn't believe in the thing any more ?

KAREN

They think he's afraid to go on ? And you ?

CARR

Do you understand him yourself ?

KAREN

Yes. But I love the queer being. I know how his mind works and his bitterness—*and* his infernal humility.

CARR

Humility ! Isn't it pride ?

KAREN

It's not his prestige he's thinking about. And not the job. That's where you're on the wrong track. You expect him to care about being the famous man who saved the world. Anyhow, you think he ought to want to save the world. Well, he doesn't. He doesn't give a farthing for the world's comfort—or his own. They can use his Scorpions or not—that's their affair. What he does care about—as an artist cares about his art—is mathematical truth. That is absolute. That's a religion. He won't go back on it. (*A pause.*) But it's going back on him. (*She says this in such acute personal distress that* CARR *moves across and puts a fatherly hand on her.*)

CARR

What is it that's on your mind ?

KAREN

He might lose faith in himself.

CARR

That's not your fault.

KAREN

Isn't it ? He thinks I doubt him. Brissing, Dick— now me. He found me the other day going through old calculations and he said : " Well, Karen, have you found the howler ? " He thought I was looking for it.

CARR

Were you ?

KAREN

I was going through *his* calculations—and my brother's —the ones I hadn't a share in.

CARR

But what for ?

KAREN

The joy of it—like a gallery of masterpieces. He didn't believe that. And if now—(*she shakes her head violently*)—I daren't—I daren't do anything that would make him believe I doubted him.

CARR

Why should you?

KAREN

There's one chance to save this place.

CARR

There was. He didn't take it. He won't now.

KAREN

There's still one chance. (*Enter* DENHAM.)

DENHAM

The car's here, Miss.

CARR

I'll escape by the verandah. Give us a word when she's gone. I don't want to blunder in on her. (*Exit* CARR *by verandah.* DENHAM *shows in* LADY HELSTON.)

DENHAM

Lady Helston, Miss. (*Exit* DENHAM. KAREN *rises to meet her.*)

LADY HELSTON

I wasn't sure you'd want to see me.

KAREN

The message was : you wanted to see me. I wondered why.

LADY HELSTON

I am leaving for England to-morrow morning.

KAREN

So I heard. . . . Shall we sit down ?

LADY HELSTON

For a moment. Why in this room ?

KAREN

If you came to triumph, I thought you'd like it. If you came to apologize, it's suitable too.

LADY HELSTON

I haven't come for either.

KAREN

I know. You came because you couldn't help it. Isn't that true ?

LADY HELSTON

As a matter of fact, I had made up a perfectly good conventional excuse for coming, but I suppose I needn't trouble you with it.

KAREN

That must be the straightest thing you've ever said. I like you for that.

LADY HELSTON

I only thought that as we aren't likely to meet again—

KAREN

(Steadily and without rhetoric)

And as you will never be in this room again, and as you did something here that twists and torments you, and as you don't know whether you're glad or sorry or a misunderstood woman or a cad—because you are in a hopeless tangle and curious and on edge—you had to come here, and see me, and see this room once more, and find out what your sensations were.

LADY HELSTON

(Puzzled and a little frightened by a mood and method she does not understand)

Are you pitying me?

KAREN

I am talking about what happens to interest me at the moment. I wondered why you'd come. Now I know. You wanted a scene to wipe out the memory of the last. Do you lie awake at nights wishing you could get back to the bridge table and play a hand again?

LADY HELSTON

(Not alive to her irony)

Why, do you?

KAREN

I don't play bridge.

LADY HELSTON

You are an extraordinary woman!

231

KAREN

Because I don't play bridge ?

LADY HELSTON

You don't like anything I like.

KAREN

I do.   Men.

LADY HELSTON

But you can't *say* that !

KAREN

I can to a woman I shall never see again.   Doesn't it even interest you ?   Doesn't anything *real* interest you ? Here I am.   I took the man you wanted, and you have ruined what I care for more than anything on earth.   I think you are a cad and you think I'm a slut, and somehow we both think we're right.   No one's the villainess in her own story.   Two utterly different human beings— neither with imagination enough to see the other's point of view.   And in about three minutes by the clock, when you go out of that door, we shall be dead to each other— as if we really were dead.   We might as well tell the truth meanwhile.

LADY HELSTON

I don't know what you're talking about.   If I'd had any idea you would behave like this, I wouldn't have come.

KAREN

How did you think I'd behave ?

232

LADY HELSTON

I thought you might be angry.

KAREN

You'd have enjoyed that.

LADY HELSTON

Or we might——

KAREN

A reconciliation scene? Did you really think that?

LADY HELSTON

No. (*She means "yes".*) But we might have talked.

KAREN

Aren't we talking? And you would have sat there purring over your little drama. Somehow you'd have found out what you want to know. I'll tell you. I'm not his mistress and never have been.

LADY HELSTON

I don't think I care.

KAREN

What *do* you care about—really care?

LADY HELSTON

I loved him.

KAREN
(*Just a denial*)

No.

LADY HELSTON

I loved him—horribly.

KAREN

(*Dead hard*)

You believe that's true !

LADY HELSTON

It is. (*With sudden spirit, rising*) My God, you are
arrogant ! Do you think no one can love but yourself ?
(*They are now both standing, face to face,* KAREN *on* L. *and*
LADY HELSTON *on* R., *looking towards the Control Room.*)

KAREN

(*In astonishment*)

Then it is true. You did love him. We don't speak
the same language, that's all. We are two women,
but not the same animal. Love means power to you.
Vanity—no, that's not fair. *Power*—over him.

LADY HELSTON

Why is that wrong ? It's natural. It's you who
are unnatural. Because you have brains, you want to
submit yourself. That's love to you. You want to be
ordered—under his discipline. If he hit you, you'd take
that. Wouldn't you ?

KAREN

Yes, I would.

LADY HELSTON

(*Without venom—a statement of fact as she sees it*)

That's why you're a slut. And why you didn't save
him.

KAREN

I want power *from* him. I want to be more and more myself because I love him more and more. Is that being a slut?

LADY HELSTON

I wanted more and more power over him because I loved him more and more. Is that being a cad?

KAREN

Perhaps the little words don't mean much in the end.

LADY HELSTON

I'll go. (*She reaches entrance to verandah.*)

KAREN

Why didn't I save him?

LADY HELSTON

Because you submit. Because you didn't dare. (*Exit* LADY HELSTON. *After a moment* KAREN *goes to door* R. *and opens it to call in the others. As she does so* FERRERS *comes in by door* L., *and she turns back to meet him.*)

FERRERS

Disposed of? I saw her go from my window. Strangely calm. Did she come to enjoy another scene? Who played the lead in this one?

KAREN

I think it played itself.

FERRERS

Where are the others ?

KAREN

In the mess-room.   They'll come back.

FERRERS

I'll go then.

KAREN

Why ?

FERRERS

They go over things, Karen.

KAREN

Or are you afraid ?

FERRERS

Of them ?

KAREN

Of me.

FERRERS

You !

KAREN

Do you know I love you ?

FERRERS

My dear——

KAREN

I wonder if you do.   Do you know I believe in you ?

FERRERS

Perhaps you love me too much.

236

KAREN

No. I believe in you—in your work.

FERRERS
(*Non-committal*)

Thank you.

KAREN

But remember. I said : " I believe in you ". Remember that.

FERRERS

I will.

KAREN

Whatever comes, remember. (BRISSING, CARR *and* SANDFORD *come in* R. FERRERS *at once goes out* L.)

CARR

Ferrers ! . . . Get him back.

KAREN

No. Leave him.

CARR

We have sighted the First Lord.

KAREN

Alone ? (SANDFORD *begins to put the room straight and rings bell.*)

CARR

And on foot.

KAREN

Coming here ?

CARR

He is here—with Brissing. We must have Ferrers.

KAREN

Not yet.

CARR

But——

KAREN

No. Please. Not yet. Take it from me. (BRISSING *shows in* FIRST LORD *from the verandah.* DENHAM *enters* R. *He stands and waits for orders.*)

FIRST LORD

I hope I don't intrude. I've come to pay a call on the Mess.

CARR

Come in, sir.

FIRST LORD

Thank you. I walked up. Air and exercise. The Admiral and the Flag Captain are following in the car. We timed it to meet here as nearly as we could.

SANDFORD

What will you have, sir ?

FIRST LORD

Thank you. It was rather a long walk. A gin and tonic.

SANDFORD

(*To* DENHAM)

And some whiskey.

DENHAM

Yes, sir. (*Exit.*)

FIRST LORD

There's talk of a signal station on Flag Point. The Admiral thought we might have a look at it. Is it a pretty place ?

BRISSING

A cigarette, sir.

FIRST LORD

A pipe if I may. It persuades the newspapers that, though uninspiring, one is English at heart. For the same reason, if statesmen must go to France, it's advisable for them to cut out Paris and go straight to Aix-les-Bains. (*There is an awkward pause and the* FIRST LORD *continues to make conversation.*) You have some remarkable bougainvillias in your garden. Your cultivation, Miss Selby ?

KAREN

No, sir. This—(BRISSING)—is the gardener.

FIRST LORD

(*To* BRISSING)

I congratulate you. Gunnery and gardens. And what do you do in your spare time ?

BRISSING

If we get long leave after this, I mean to spend a bit of it in France.

FIRST LORD

At Aix-les-Bains, I hope.

BRISSING

No. With a car, very slowly through Burgundy.

FIRST LORD

I shouldn't inform the Admiralty if I were you. It's dangerous in England to give an impression that you like the French for their own sake. It throws suspicion on your morals. (DENHAM *comes in and hands drinks.*)

SANDFORD

We shall get leave after this, shan't we, sir ?

FIRST LORD

I'll take your orders. Lieutenant-Commander Brissing—Burgundy. And what after that ?

BRISSING

Whale Island. Then a big ship.

FIRST LORD
(*To* SANDFORD)

And you ?

SANDFORD

I'd like China.

FIRST LORD

They may have less oriental ideas at the Admiralty, but I'll see it through. (*To* CARR) Have you any instructions?

CARR

I shall retire.

FIRST LORD

Why, may I ask?

CARR

Oh, not because of this. Family reasons.

FIRST LORD

I'm glad. No one must take a personal view of this—or of anything arising from the public service. I want there to be no bitterness if I can avoid it. You are probably asking yourselves questions.

CARR

There's one I'm always asking myself. Isn't there a kind of paradox in it all? If Ferrers had admitted that his calculations were wrong, you'd have let the show go forward. The Admiral said as much. So did you, sir, this morning. But because he knows he's right and says so, you close down on us. Sounds mad to me.

FIRST LORD

Gilbertian, Carr, not mad. We live in a democracy and democracy is always charitable to fools, but not to arrogant genius. It's quite simple. You can back a man who has made a mistake, but not a man who won't

admit it. In one case—granted you believe in the man
—there's the hope of remedy ; in the other, not.

CARR

But Ferrers has admitted a detonator defect.

FIRST LORD

That might go on for ever. First one minor defect,
then another, and all the time his basic calculations may
be wrong.

KAREN

But if he *is* right ?

FIRST LORD

The Admiralty would say it's a big " if ".

KAREN

And you ?

FIRST LORD

I am the Admiralty for the time being. . . . But I
should like your answer to that question, Carr. Do you
believe Ferrers is right ?

CARR

Absolutely.

FIRST LORD

You are a family man. You have children. One
daughter in particular ?

CARR
(*Astonished*)

Yes, sir.

FIRST LORD

Would you stake her future on your answer to that question ?   The Admiralty, you know, has more at stake than that.   Would you ?

CARR
(*Having considered*)

I would.

FIRST LORD

And you, Sandford ?

SANDFORD

I haven't a daughter, sir.

FIRST LORD

Few men can be sure of that ; and they perhaps are not to be envied.   The question stands.

SANDFORD

Well.   (*Looks uneasily at* KAREN.)   I'm not a mathematician, sir.

FIRST LORD

Nor am I.   I have my advisers.   So have you— Ferrers and Miss Selby.   The question still stands, for me and for you.

SANDFORD

Well, sir, the point is——

FIRST LORD

Thank you.   The question is answered. . . . (*To* CARR) You see, Carr, Whitehall is not the only place.

Mr. Brissing has gone to consult the weather. If only I could sometimes do that during question-time in the House !

BRISSING
(Turns round—with the aggressiveness of a man who has ceased to be sure of himself)

I'm not trying to shirk. I've believed in Ferrers through thick and thin. You can't help it if you work with him. If he said " Work on with me until we *do* get this thing right ", I'd be with him——

FIRST LORD
" Until we *do* ", Brissing ! " Un*til* we do ? " Then it's not right ?

BRISSING
You're too quick, sir. You catch up my words. I didn't say it was wrong.

FIRST LORD
(Doubtfully)

No. But you did say that if Ferrers asked you to work on while he corrected his present error, you would stand by him. That is the Admiralty's point of view. *(Almost in anguish)* But he will admit no error in himself —no possibility of error in his own work. *(Stands up.)* Miss Selby will admit none. *(Enter* FERRERS, L. *He is nervous and suspicious.)*

FERRERS
You, sir ? I didn't know you were here. *(Angry)* Why wasn't I told ? Am I still in command here or a fool to be humoured ?

FIRST LORD

I asked them not to disturb you.

FERRERS

I see.   I'm sorry.   Afraid I'm on edge.   (*Trying to be ordinary*) What is it Miss Selby won't admit ?

FIRST LORD

That there's any mistake in your calculations.

FERRERS

Incredible.   Did you ask her ?

FIRST LORD

I was on the point of asking her when you came in.

FERRERS

Pity you didn't.   The others think I'm a fool.   Not Carr, but the others.   I know that.   But my bridge is still first-rate !   That's a proof of mathematical genius all the world can understand !   I'm lucky, really.   A poet can't recommend himself to the mob unless he dies or writes cracker mottoes.   (*He looks round wildly at the grave faces regarding this cheap petulance.   Then with a quiet despair, no longer bitter, he adds, to the* FIRST LORD) Heigh-ho !   That's how they all talk, isn't it, sir ?

FIRST LORD

Who ?

FERRERS

The poor devils who were ALMOST—and just hadn't got it in 'em.

KAREN

Don't say that !   Don't !

FERRERS

That's what it comes to, doesn't it ?

KAREN

Oh my God !   I wish they *had* asked me that question.   Why did you come in ?   I'm such a coward for you.   (DENHAM *shows in* ADMIRAL *and* FLAG CAPTAIN *and goes out.*)

ADMIRAL

We had trouble with the self-starter.   How are you, Ferrers.   I wish you'd invent one that worked.   (*To* FIRST LORD) We haven't kept you ?

FIRST LORD

I've had a most interesting talk.   Sandford is going to China.   Brissing, I'm afraid, is going to France.

FLAG CAPTAIN
(*Heavily affable*)

I wish all First Lords took as much interest in personnel.

ADMIRAL

We'd better go while the going's good. . . . Pretty well cleared up, Carr ?

CARR

Most of the important things, sir.

ADMIRAL

Good. Well, we must be off. Are you set, Harrowby?

FIRST LORD

Good-bye then, gentlemen. (*They say good-bye to him.*) Good-bye, Ferrers.

FERRERS

It's a queer business. You're right; so am I. I should do what you are doing; you'd do what I am. And we both know it.

FIRST LORD

Thank you, Ferrers. Good-bye, Miss Selby. Do you remember what Pompey said to Menas in the galley? . . . That's a pity. (*Hesitates.*) Good-bye.

KAREN
(*Loud, forced, unnatural*)

There's something I must say. (*They all look at her; the* ADMIRAL *at his watch.*)

ADMIRAL

We ought to get on.

FLAG CAPTAIN

If we're to be at Flag Point by tea-time we must.

KAREN

I ought to have said this before.

247

ADMIRAL

I'm sure, Miss Selby, you don't wish to delay the First Lord.

KAREN
(*To* FIRST LORD)
Shall you be here again ?

FIRST LORD
Never.

KAREN
Then I must say it now.

FLAG CAPTAIN
Really, is it of such importance ?

FIRST LORD
I think, perhaps, it is.

KAREN
I'd rather say it to you alone.

FIRST LORD
No, Miss Selby. Whatever it is, the Admiral and the Flag Captain must hear it.

KAREN
I mean—not Ferrers.

FERRERS
Not me !

FIRST LORD
(*Gently*)
Will it not have to be said to him some time ?

248

KAREN
(*Struggling*)

I suppose so.   So be it.

FIRST LORD

A moment, please.   I think we should like to sit down.   (*They all sit except* FERRERS *and* KAREN.)   Now.

KAREN
(*Looks at them all.   Suddenly takes* FERRERS' *hand*)
I have found a defect in the basic formula.

FERRERS
(*Wrenching himself away*)
What in God's name do you mean ?

KAREN
(*Louder*)
I have found a defect in your basic formula.

FLAG CAPTAIN
(*Springing up*)
You can't say that at this time of day.

KAREN

I do.

FLAG CAPTAIN

Why not before ?

KAREN
(*To* ADMIRAL)
Since your report was sent in, I have gone over Ferrers' calculations again.

249

FERRERS

That's what you were spying for.

KAREN

(*Disregarding him*)

Two months.   Line by line.

FLAG CAPTAIN

And you found this error, when?   Since lunch?
Why couldn't you tell us at the inquiry this morning?

FIRST LORD

(*Quickly intervening, for she is at a loss*)

One must make allowances for human nature, Flag
Captain.   I think she has had a great—confidence in
him.   You might perhaps hesitate yourself to disagree
openly with the Admiral.   You would, no doubt, speak
at last if the interests of the Service required it.   But you
would hesitate, would you not?

FERRERS

What's wrong with the formula?   Where is it
wrong?   You see, she can't answer that.

FIRST LORD

(*Again giving her time*)

It is of course a question she will have to answer
when the time comes.   There are many highly complex matters which——

KAREN

I can answer it.

FIRST LORD

(*Gratefully abandoning his improvised oration*)

Can you ?   I'm delighted to hear that.

KAREN

(*Very fast*)

I found the error by examining afresh the whole of the vibration experiments on which the formula was based. From these he deduced a vibration-constant which he called K.   K itself *is* constant, but in calculating vibration-effect, you have to apply a correction that depends on the density of the atmosphere.   The trouble is with that correction.   It is——

FIRST LORD

Greek to us, Miss Selby.   The question is : Can it be put right ?

KAREN

Not by me.

FIRST LORD

Not ?

KAREN

He could.

FIRST LORD

I see.

ADMIRAL

Ferrers, is this new to you ?

FERRERS

New !   (*To* KAREN) We have tested those experimental results again and again—together.

KAREN

I tested some. You tested some. It wasn't always a double check.

FERRERS

If mine were wrong, how could they have locked with yours ? They fitted group by group like the dogs of a clutch. (*Now with entreaty close to her ; his own confidence shaken.*) Tell me. Forget all these people. They lie. We all do. Mathematics doesn't. You have worked with me. I trust you. You *do* know. Tell me. Am I all wrong ?

KAREN

You are wrong.

FERRERS

How deep does it go ?

KAREN

(*Lying desperately*)

Very deep.

FERRERS

(*Turns from her*)

Then everything goes. If what is true is proved a lie, nothing is left.

KAREN

Remember. Remember. Remember.

FERRERS

Remember what ? I've often wondered—what it would feel like to think you're sane, to know you are, and then to have it proved that you're mad.

KAREN

But this can be put right.

FERRERS

Unless I'm mad, there's nothing to put right. If there is, I'm mad. (*He comes away from them all, right down stage.*) Madness and sanity are two intersecting circles. Suddenly they close on the same centre. Poor Charles Lamb knew that. So the world spins. (*Fiercely, at her*) Did you never learn that in your astronomy? (*He remains apart from them.*)

FIRST LORD
(*Seizing* KAREN'S *arm*)

No, girl, leave him. Leave him a little while. He'll come back.

FLAG CAPTAIN

We're no forrader.

ADMIRAL

How—no forrader?

FLAG CAPTAIN
(*Contemptuously*)

Ferrers is no good. Use your eyes. Gibbering like a lunatic. He's thrown his hand in.

FERRERS
(*Passionately*)

Not to you!

FIRST LORD

Allow me. Commander Ferrers: As long as we, who are not good at sums, were saying " It's you who

253

are wrong ", you told us to go to hell.   That I can understand—the natural instinct of an expert.   In my own
case, in so far as I have expert knowledge of anything,
it is of cats.

BRISSING

Did you say " cats ", sir ?

FIRST LORD

I did undoubtedly say " cats ", sir.   A pacific taste,
you may think, in a First Lord of the Admiralty ; but
you must understand that I have not always been First
Lord of the Admiralty and shall not always be.   The
Captains and the Kings depart, but the cat is, philosophic-
ally speaking, always on the mat.   (*To* FERRERS) I have
an unsurpassed knowledge of them, and if a group of old
women told me I was wrong and that I must re-examine
all my data and rewrite all my monographs on the subject, I should tell them—I should neglect their advice.
But there is one lady with whom I conduct what may be
called a feline correspondence and whose opinion I respect.   If she were to tell me I was wrong in some
particular, I should not rest until I had, so to speak,
re-examined and perhaps reconstructed my whole feline
theory.   You get my drift, Ferrers ?

FERRERS

What is it you want, sir ?   I'll consent to anything.

FIRST LORD

Nothing but this : your undertaking to go into Miss

Selby's case with an open mind. (*Shrewdly*) You might, meanwhile, reposition the detonator mechanism.

FLAG CAPTAIN

What does this mean? You don't intend to go on!

FIRST LORD

Certainly.

FLAG CAPTAIN

With Ferrers in this state?

FIRST LORD

I had a friend once. He was a great artist. His canvas was burned. That night he was mad—like a child with fever. Next morning, he began to paint again.

FLAG CAPTAIN

But this needs a decision of the Board of Admiralty as a whole.

FIRST LORD

It does.

FLAG CAPTAIN

Wedgcroft won't stand for it.

FIRST LORD
(*Stern*)

No? I must ask him to breakfast. (*Silky again.*) If Admiral Helston sees fit to write amendments to his report, I will countersign them. There should be no great difficulty. You are with me, Admiral?

ADMIRAL

I am responsible on the spot, sir. We are working in the dark. If a new series of experiments were to fail, what answer could I give?

FLAG CAPTAIN

It's we who should be blamed. The naval members of the Board won't put up with it.

ADMIRAL

I agree, Winter. We've gone too far. (*To* FIRST LORD) I can't go back, sir.

FIRST LORD

Admiral Helston——

ADMIRAL

I can't go back, sir. It's no longer a technical question with me. It's a question of character.

FLAG CAPTAIN

Character, after all, is more important than brains.

FIRST LORD

How many battles have been lost under that motto!

ADMIRAL

I'm a plain seaman, sir. I have made my report. I stand by it.

FIRST LORD

Then I accept your report, Admiral. It shall be pigeon-holed with honour. Your brother-in-law will respect you for it. And I shall overrule it. . . . Now, we shall be late at Flag Point. (*To* CARR) You have a car? Why don't you three officers come with us? Miss Selby?

KAREN

I'd rather stay.

FIRST LORD

Good-bye, then. You have deserved your privilege. Mr. Brissing will show me his bougainvillias as we go. (ADMIRAL *and* FLAG-CAPTAIN *go out.* FERRERS, *who is wishing only to be alone, has turned away.* FIRST LORD *approaches him as if to say good-bye, but decides to leave him.*) Well, we shall meet again. (CARR *and* SANDFORD *go out. The* FIRST LORD *takes* BRISSING *with him through door. As he goes :*) Burgundy will have to wait, but good wine matures in bottle.

FERRERS

Why didn't you tell me? You must have known long, long ago. You spoke of it to them as if it were a slip in arithmetic. The correction to K! (*She tries to speak.*) You knew well enough. " Very deep ", you said. Very deep! I should think so! If that's wrong, everything that depends on it is utterly wrong. It can't be put right. That old fool goes off saying he'll give me time. He can give me eternity. The whole thing falls down.

KAREN

Listen to me.

FERRERS

The calculations locked! Madness and sanity are

257

intersecting circles. Now they run together. The corrections to K belong to the early groups, and after that everything locked !

KAREN

Stop.   For one minute stop and listen to me.

FERRERS

Proofs are not proofs.   Certainty isn't certainty. Mathematics do lie.   They lie and deceive like human beings.

KAREN

I was lying then.

FERRERS

Nothing is absolute.   (*Looking at her*) Nothing is true. (*Thrusting her away from him. Very quietly*) Who are you ?   Why are you kneeling there ?   Sometimes, when you are awake in bed, thinking, between waking and sleeping, your thought runs quieter and quieter, like a still, flashing stream, like truth itself without reason, and you glide down that stream knowing that at the end of it —then suddenly there's a click of your mind, the shutter of a camera, and it's all gone—all gone—all gone—and the little rat Reason is gnawing inside your head again.

KAREN

Come back.   Come back !

FERRERS

Who are you ?   Why are you kneeling there ?   There was a madman once who wrote—do you remember ?—

258

" If ever in my solitary room
  I in an ecstasy should lie
  And God's own touch have put my Fool to sleep,
  Out of his sleep, my aching Fool would cry
  ' Ask : where is truth ? ' and I should ask and creep
  Out of my vision into Reason's gloom."

(*A triumphant cry*) He was happy, the man who wrote that ! He knew how the world spins ! (*Enter* FIRST LORD.) (*In a changed voice—a man waking*) Who is that ? (*Seizing her hands*) Karen, speak to me.

FIRST LORD
My pipe. I left it.

FERRERS
(*Recognizing him*)
I thought you had gone to England.

FIRST LORD
To England ! (*Perceiving that something desperate is wrong. To* KAREN) What is it ?

KAREN
I don't know yet.

FERRERS
(*Almost back again from the place to which he has been*)
The old cove has lost his pipe. Where is it ?

FIRST LORD
I presume you were lying, Miss Selby ?

KAREN

How soon did you know?

FIRST LORD

A little before you began.

KAREN

What did Pompey say to Menas in the galley?

FIRST LORD

"In me, 'tis villainy; in thee, it *has* been good service."

FERRERS

Lying about what?

FIRST LORD

There is no fault in your calculations, Ferrers.

FERRERS

I know that. . . . Oh, I remember, I remember, I remember. (*To* KAREN) You said there was. Why did you say that? If I had believed you, it would have driven me mad. (*Enter* BRISSING).

BRISSING

The Admiral suggests, sir, that if you have found your pipe, as Flag Point is some distance away——

260

FIRST LORD

Did he suggest it as courteously as that? (*To* KAREN) Statesmen and women must do what they can to save men of genius from men of character. (*Exit* FIRST LORD.)

FERRERS

Now the old boy has said his piece, we can get on.

KAREN

My dear, rest a little.

FERRERS

Rest? Why?

KAREN

Because, very nearly, you have been——

FERRERS

What? Mad? Odd you should say that. There was a click in my mind, like the shutter of a camera. And a stream flashing. (*A sharp order*) Get Sandford back. (*She does not move. He takes her hand, kisses it.*) Thank you, my dear. I know. (*As she makes no answer, he looks up and finds her gazing at him.*) What is it?

KAREN

You said "Thank you". You said "I know". What did you know? (*He hesitates.*) Say it. Please say it.

FERRERS

When I shook, you held steady.   When I failed, you did not despise me.   That's a new world for me.

KAREN

You were lost and gone away.   Useless.   Mad.   I held you.

FERRERS

Not a god.

KAREN

Like a boy with sunstroke.

FERRERS

Not your master.

KAREN

Always ; but then—asleep.

FERRERS

(*Slowly, looking* into *her with profound curiosity*)
I have never seen you asleep.   The battle goes out of people then.   (*Suddenly, like a pistol*) I love you, Karen. I love *you.*

KAREN

I love you with all my heart.   (*He takes her in his arms, never moving his eyes from her face, but does not kiss her.   She shows him her key.*)   Is this mine now?

262

FERRERS

Will you have it ?

KAREN

It frightens me still.

FERRERS

Will you have it ?

KAREN

Yes, please. . . . Please God.

FERRERS

And don't leave it sculling about. (*Her hands and all her strength close over it.*)

KAREN

To have and to hold.

FERRERS

" My head. My head." What ? I've heard that.

KAREN

It was the Shunnamite's boy in the Bible. He had sunstroke.

FERRERS

(*Without personal application*)

He was raised from the dead.

263

THE FLASHING STREAM

KAREN

" And the child sneezed seven times."

FERRERS

" And the child opened his eyes."

Curtain

Printed in Great Britain by R. & R. CLARK, LIMITED, *Edinburgh*